AF255822

THE SEVEN SACRED LAWS OF FEMININE POWER

Claim Your Power. Live from Your Truth.

Theresa Ream

Aurora Corialis Publishing

Pittsburgh, PA

THE SEVEN SACRED LAWS OF FEMININE POWER
Copyright © 2026 by Theresa Ream

All rights reserved. No part of this book may be used, reproduced, stored in a retrieval system, or transmitted by any means—electronic, mechanical, photocopy, microfilm, recording, or otherwise—without written permission from the publisher, except in the case of brief quotations embodied in critical articles or reviews. No part of this book is to be used to train artificial intelligence. For more information, address: cori@auroracorialispublishing.com.
All external reference links utilized in this book have been validated to the best of our ability and are current as of publication.
The publisher and the author make no guarantees concerning the level of success you may experience by following the advice and strategies contained in this book, and you accept the risk that results will differ for each individual.
Neither the authors nor the publisher assumes any responsibility for errors, omissions, or contrary interpretations of the subject matter herein. Any perceived slight of an individual or organization is purely unintentional.
To ensure privacy and confidentiality, some names or other identifying characteristics of the persons included in this book may have been changed. All the personal examples of the authors' own lives and experiences have not been altered.

Printed in the United States of America
Edited by: Allison Hrip, Aurora Corialis Publishing
Paperback ISBN: 978-1-958481-74-5
Ebook ISBN: 978-1-958481-75-2

Table of Contents

Preface i

How to Read This Book iii

Introduction to The Seven Laws of Feminine Power 1

Chapter One: The Law of Embodying Your Unique Abilities and Gifts 7

Chapter Two: The Law of Turning Your Imperfections into Power 31

Chapter Three: The Law of Allies and Amplifiers 55

Chapter Four: The Law of Alchemizing Your Gifts 77

Chapter Five: The Law of Protecting Your Power 99

Chapter Six: The Law of Feminine Flow— Dancing with Life's Rhythm 119

Chapter Seven: The Law of Feminine Leadership—Leading with Grace 141

Closing Prayer 161

Preface

There once was a woman. A smart, accomplished businesswoman. She was learned and capable, respected by her peers, admired for her advice, and known for her wisdom. She had built a solid life … and a name for herself. She knew much about many things, but there was one thing she hadn't yet learned: how to believe in herself. She could teach strategy, solve problems, and give brilliant counsel to others. But when she looked in the mirror, she couldn't see her own brilliance. She had knowledge, but not embodiment. Wisdom, but not ownership. Even with all her experience, all her intuition, and all her skill, she still couldn't see her true power. She had become a walking library, full of information for others to borrow. A keeper of lessons others came to harvest, while she stood quietly in the background, the curator of other people's breakthroughs.

She missed the point of it all. She missed the sacred truth that her gifts were never meant to be stored; they were meant to be lived, passed to others, and given in service. She was not just the keeper of learning; she was the learning itself. And that woman? She lives in each of us. She lives in the boardroom executive who hides her intuition, the mother who has set aside her own dreams, the entrepreneur who builds for others but not for herself. She lives in the woman who knows she is powerful but hasn't permitted herself to become that power. So, I ask you today, are you simply the storage for all that you've learned? Or have you become all that you've learned? Because there is so much power in you: deep, vast, and waiting. You have been given gifts, insights, and experiences that no one else in this world possesses in quite the same way. It's time to wake them up. To revel in them. To live them. When you finally believe—when that sacred moment of revelation arrives—you'll see that everything you've lived, everything you've learned, and everything you've been has prepared you for this moment: the moment you step into your power, the moment you begin to fly. And through these Seven Sacred Laws of Feminine Power, you will rise ... not by learning or doing more, but by finally becoming all that you already know.

How to Read This Book

The Seven Laws of Feminine Power is not meant to be rushed through like a traditional book. It is written to be experienced, reflected on, and embodied. These laws are not simply ideas to understand with your mind; they are principles meant to live within you and shape the way you move through the world.

You may notice that certain themes and concepts appear more than once throughout the chapters. This is intentional. True transformation rarely happens from hearing something once. It happens through repetition, reflection, and practice. Each time an idea returns, it offers you another layer of understanding and another opportunity to see it within your own life.

Rather than reading quickly, allow yourself to pause. Notice what resonates. Journal, reflect, and return to sections that speak to you. Some chapters may feel immediately familiar, while others may reveal their meaning over time.

Think of this book less as something to finish and more as something to return to. Each reading will meet you at a different stage of your journey. As you grow, the laws will deepen with you.

These pages are an invitation to remember your power, embody it, and lead from it.

Introduction to The Seven Laws of Feminine Power

You Were Born Powerful. Now It's Time to Lead That Way

There comes a moment in every woman's life when pretending stops. When she grows tired of shrinking herself, tired of trying to fit into spaces never meant to hold her brilliance, tired of the masks, the appeasing, the proving. A moment when something inside her whispers: *There must be more than this.*

When we finally listen, that moment marks the beginning of true power.

If you're holding this book, it's likely because that moment has arrived for you.

It may have come quietly, during a sleepless night or a tearful drive. It may have arrived after years of success that still didn't fulfill. Or perhaps it came as a sudden knowing, a fierce wave of clarity that something had to change, and that something was *you* finally coming home to yourself.

This book is an invitation to walk through that door. To step into your true power not by doing more, hustling harder, or perfecting yourself, but by becoming more of *you*.

This is a return. A reclamation. A remembrance.

You were born powerful. Now it's time to lead that way.

Feminine Power Is Not a Performance; it's a Presence

We've been taught that power looks like force. That it's earned through exhaustion, dominance, perfection, and endless doing. That to be taken seriously, a woman must suppress her softness, harden her edges, and outwork everyone in the room.

But that model of power is unsustainable, and frankly, untrue.

Feminine power is different. It doesn't roar to be heard. It doesn't conquer to be seen. It doesn't chase applause or shape-shift to stay acceptable. Feminine power is not loud, but it is unmistakable. It doesn't compete; it commands. It doesn't perform; it resonates.

You don't have to abandon yourself to be powerful. In fact, your power lives in your presence, your intuition, your softness, your boundaries, your joy, and your embodiment. It lives in your ability to lead without leaving yourself behind.

That is the kind of power we're awakening here.

Power Is Not Taken; It's Remembered and Reclaimed

We often think of power as something to fight for, to gain through external achievements or validation. But the truth is, your personal power is already within you. You don't need to steal it, earn it, or wait for someone else to give it to you. You only need to remember where you've placed it, and why you ever forgot.

So many women don't realize the immense gifts they already carry. The wisdom they've earned through lived experience. The intuition they've silenced. The talents they've dismissed or downplayed. The boundaries they've neglected to set. The energy they've spent proving instead of owning.

This book will help you identify your personal power assets, those unique strengths, abilities, and qualities that are already yours. And you'll learn to use them in ways that create real, lasting success in your business, your relationships, your finances, and your soul.

Transformation doesn't happen by adding layers; it happens by peeling them away. By honoring who you've always been beneath the social conditioning.

The Seven Laws of Feminine Power

Throughout these pages, you'll be introduced to seven sacred principles, laws that govern your personal power, your feminine wisdom, and your ability to lead and live with authenticity.

These are not rules to obey; they are deep truths to return to. They are energetic frameworks to support your embodiment. They are invitations to align your outer success with your inner knowing.

The Seven Laws

1. **The Law of Embodying Your Unique Abilities and Gifts**
    Discover your innate gifts and how to lead from the core of who you are.
2. **The Law of Turning Your Imperfections into Power**
    Turn your perceived flaws into your most magnetic qualities.
3. **The Law of Allies and Amplifiers**
    Surround yourself with those who reflect your greatness and help you rise.
4. **The Law of Alchemizing Your Gifts**
    Set sacred boundaries, protect your energy, and honor your purpose fiercely.
5. **The Law of Protecting Your Power**
    Safeguard your energy, honor your boundaries, and build aligned prosperity by offering what is most authentic to you.

6. **The Law of Feminine Flow**
   Learn to dance with life, embrace your cycles, and trust your rhythm.
7. **The Law of Feminine Leadership**
   Step fully into leadership by trusting your inner voice and radiating influence.

Each chapter will guide you through reflection, embodiment, and action. You'll find prompts to help you integrate the material, stories that speak to your soul, and tools to anchor these truths into your everyday life.

These are not just ideas; they are practices for how to live, love, and lead powerfully.

This Is Personal Power Reclaimed and Redefined. It's Yours to Claim.

No more chasing, pleasing, or proving.

No more waiting for the perfect moment or permission.

No more abandoning the very parts of you that hold your magic.

This is the season of return. Of reconnection. Of reclamation. It is you, redefined.

This book will not give you something you don't already have. What it will do is help you remember. Remember who you were before the world told you who to be. Remember the truth you've tucked away. Remember the version of you that doesn't need to shrink, explain, or justify.

You already have everything you need.

You've always had it.

Now it's time to explore, expand, and lead from your place of power. This book is a safe place to begin to do all those things.

I invite you to show up fully. Bring your heart, your hurt, your wisdom, your wonder, your voice, and your softness. Bring your boldness and your brilliance. Bring the part of you that you've dimmed. Bring the woman you've hidden and the leader you're becoming. Bring the powerful woman you were born to be.

The world is not waiting for another copy of someone else. It is waiting for the real, powerful, radiant, unfiltered, and unmistakable you.

Let's begin.

Chapter One: The Law of Embodying Your Unique Abilities and Gifts

"Your personal power doesn't come from force, but from your abilities, knowledge, and the ideas you present to the world."
~ Theresa Ream

The Power Within You

Your abilities are the foundation of your personal power. They shape your influence, impact, and opportunities. Yet, many people overlook their own strengths, focusing instead on external validation or societal expectations. Identifying your abilities is not just about recognizing what you're good at; it's about understanding how you add value to the world and leveraging your unique skills to build a life of purpose and success.

The process of identifying your abilities begins with self-awareness. By taking an honest inventory of your natural talents, learned skills, and hidden strengths, you can begin to see where your true power lies. This chapter will guide you through this process, helping you discover what makes you uniquely capable and how to use those abilities to your advantage.

What Are Your Abilities?

Abilities come in many forms. Some are tangible, like painting, writing, or public speaking. Others are intangible, like emotional intelligence, resilience, or strategic thinking. The first step in identifying your abilities is to broaden your perspective on what counts as a valuable skill and/or ability.

Types of Skills and Abilities

1. **Natural Talents**
   These are the skills that come effortlessly to you. Perhaps you have a sharp intuition, a gift for storytelling, or an innate sense of leadership.

2. **Learned Skill**
   These are the abilities you have acquired through education, training, or experience. They may include coding, legal expertise, marketing, or financial analysis.

3. **Social Skills**
   These include being a great conversationalist, a skilled networker, or an empathetic listener. These abilities often translate into strong relationships and increase influence.

4. **Creative Abilities**
   You might be a talented musician, poet, or designer. Creativity isn't just about artistry, though; it's about thinking outside the box and finding innovative solutions.

5. **Strategic Thinking**
   Some people naturally excel at problem-solving, planning, and seeing the bigger picture. These skills are invaluable in leadership and business.

6. **Emotional Strengths**
   Resilience, adaptability, and patience are often overlooked but are crucial abilities that can drive long-term success.

Leveraging Your Abilities for Power and Influence

"Stop shrinking to fit places you've already outgrown. Your power was never meant to be comfortable; it was meant to be transformational."
~ Theresa Ream

In this chapter, you will begin to identify skills and abilities through exercises and reflection. The next step is to learn how to use them strategically. (Don't worry, I will include examples to help guide you through this process.) Abilities on their own are valuable, but their real power comes from how you apply them to build influence, create opportunities, and shape your personal and professional life.

Turning Abilities into Assets

Monetizing Your Skills

Whether you're an expert in a particular field or have a hobby you excel at, your abilities can be turned into a source of income. Consider how best to monetize your skills in a way that makes you light up. It could be freelancing, coaching, or starting a business based on your strengths and values.

Your skills are not random; they are gifts placed within you to be cultivated, expressed, and shared. Whether you've mastered a profession, nurtured a talent, or honed a hobby that brings you joy, these abilities carry the potential to generate abundance when you choose to stand in your feminine power.

Too often, women stay in roles or jobs where their skills are used but not celebrated. You may find yourself drained by a workplace that doesn't honor your creativity, your leadership, or your desire for freedom. That's your inner knowing whispering: *It's time to create something of your own.*

Monetizing your skills isn't just about earning money; it's about aligning your energy with your purpose. Imagine designing a business that allows you to coach others through what you've mastered or launching a creative service that turns your natural strengths into impact. Maybe you've always dreamed of turning your hobby into a source of income, whether it's crafting, writing, designing, teaching, or healing. When you infuse your offerings with authenticity and passion, you attract opportunities and clients who value your uniqueness.

This is the feminine path to monetization: not hustling or forcing but creating from what already lights you up. When your skills meet your joy, and your joy meets a need in the world, you step into a flow of both prosperity and fulfillment. That's when you're no longer just working; you're *living in your power*. You will learn more about this in Chapter Four: The Law of Alchemizing Your Gifts.

Using Your Skills to Build Relationships

"The depth of your relationships shapes the richness of your life."
~ Theresa Ream

Social and emotional skills can be leveraged to create strong alliances. Being a great listener or communicator makes you an asset in both professional and personal circles.

Your skills are not only meant to create income; they are also meant to create connections. In the feminine model of power, relationships are wealth. The ability to listen deeply, communicate authentically, and hold space for others is not just a "soft skill"; it is a superpower.

Think of how magnetic it feels to be around someone who truly hears you. That's the power you hold when you lean into your social and emotional intelligence. Your presence becomes a safe place. Your words carry influence. Your ability to read energy, sense what isn't being said, and respond with empathy builds bridges where others build walls. True feminine power is relational; it thrives through connection, trust, and influence. Relationships are the currency of impact, and the way I use my gifts to nurture and expand them has shaped my life and my leadership.

Below are some examples of my social and emotional skills and how I use them to power up my relationships.

Nurturing and Feminine

I use my natural feminine attributes to consciously nurture, creating spaces where people feel valued, supported, and safe to grow. This is not just kindness; it is strategy. When people feel seen and cared for, they lean closer. Trust is bridged, and deeper alliances are born.

Relatability

One of my treasured abilities is being able to connect with people from every walk of life. Whether speaking to a CEO, a new entrepreneur, a clerk in a store, or someone navigating personal transformation, I meet people exactly where they are. This relatability creates trust, intimacy, and belonging in every circle I step into.

Strategic Thinking and Decisive Choices

Beyond connection, I bring the ability to blend mindset, business, and personal transformation into unique success plans. This skill allows me to design strategies that create lasting results for others in ways they can replicate and make their own.

Strategic thinking and strong decision-making skills make me an effective leader. Understanding how to command authority and make decisive choices strengthens my influence. Leadership in the feminine does not mean imitating authority; it means embodying it. Strategic thinking and decisive choices are not about control, but about clarity. When I understand how to command authority with grace, my influence expands naturally. True leadership presence comes from owning the room with authenticity, not force. It's the ability to see the bigger picture, make aligned decisions, and guide others with vision. When I blend strategy with intuition, I become a leader others trust to follow, not because I demand it, but because my presence inspires confidence and direction. My strategic thinking has been deeply shaped throughout my life with my husband. Walking alongside him over the years taught me how to slow down, look beyond the immediate moment, and trust the process of thoughtful decision-making. In moments when I felt uncertain or overwhelmed, his steady presence helped me find clarity and confidence. Through our shared life, conversations, and challenges, I learned how to balance intuition with logic and lead with both heart and discernment. I am profoundly grateful for the way this partnership strengthened not only my thinking, but my trust in myself as a leader.

Communication and Influence

My words carry weight because they are born of lived wisdom. As a speaker, CEO, three-time best-selling author, and contributor to magazines and newspapers, I've learned how to articulate ideas with clarity and power. Whether speaking or teaching workshops, eloquence inspires, presence attracts, and communication influences. What is your lived wisdom?

Charisma and Presence

There is a quiet power in being fully yourself. True charisma is not about being the loudest in the room or performing for attention; it's about presence. It's about showing up with sincerity, warmth, and energy that others can feel. When you are grounded in your truth, people are naturally drawn to you, not because you are trying to impress them, but because you remind them of something real within themselves.

My presence invites others to pause, breathe, and feel what's possible. It opens a space where transformation can begin, not through pressure or persuasion, but through resonance. When people feel seen, safe, and inspired in your presence, they begin to access their own clarity, courage, and potential.

This kind of influence doesn't shout. It doesn't demand. It holds space. It listens. It reflects the strength in others, even when they can't see it yet. That's the kind of presence that creates a lasting impact.

Presence is power, but not the kind that dominates. It's the kind that liberates. It creates trust, connection, and momentum. It allows others to rise in your company without needing to shrink who they are. When you embody that kind of energy, you don't just lead, you elevate.

You don't have to work hard to be magnetic; simply be fully present and fully you. The more honest and grounded you are, the more powerful your presence becomes. And in that presence, others begin to believe in what's possible for themselves.

Likeability and Connection

I believe in building relationships that last. With both clients and employees, I cultivate trust and loyalty by showing up with integrity and genuine care. These connections are the foundation of professional networks, communities, and friendships that expand far beyond business. A great personal example is that although I only have a local brick-and-mortar business, at the beginning of the pandemic, I expanded my networking nationally. I started making deep friendships with women all over the United States and Canada. This led to many opportunities. I authored three bestselling anthology books with friends I met in the networking group, The Coffee Club Divas, based in Erie, Pa. I have made many business girlfriends in the Thriving Women in Business group based in San Francisco, Calif., and The Gather Community based in Santa Cruz, Calif. Now I travel the world with the precious friends I made through networking outside my locality, and it even inspired me to create Feminine W.I.L.E.S (Women Inspired Leadership Empowering

Service) Coaching, where I have the pleasure of coaching coaches, CEOs, and entrepreneurs.

Persuasion and Perspective Shifting

I help others see new possibilities. My influence is not about convincing; it's about inviting. Through stories, teaching, and coaching, I guide my employees, coaches, and entrepreneurs to shift their perspectives, break through limitations, and step into new levels of power in both life and business.

When you are in this kind of space, something subtle but powerful happens inside you. You begin to see yourself differently. Ideas that once felt out of reach start to feel possible. The limiting stories you have been telling yourself loosen their grip, and clarity replaces doubt. You do not feel pushed or pressured. You feel seen, supported, and capable of choosing a new direction that aligns with who you truly are and where you are ready to go next.

Cultivating Personal Power

I hope that walking you through some of my abilities has brought you some clarity around your attributes. Personal power is an inner reservoir of confidence, resilience, and self-awareness woven together. Challenges will always come, but when you are anchored in your feminine power, you no longer react; you respond. Confidence allows you to step forward even when the path is uncertain. Resilience carries you through the moments that test your spirit. And self-awareness keeps you rooted in truth, ensuring you act from alignment rather than fear. Mastering these inner qualities means you are never at the mercy of circumstance; instead, you lead your life from strength, sovereignty, and choice.

It's Time to Own Your Abilities and Act

*"Knowing your abilities is an act of gratitude. It honors
the gifts you were given to uplift, create, and lead."*
~ Theresa Ream

Understanding your abilities is the first step toward building personal power. By identifying and leveraging your strengths, you take control of your life and shape your path with intention. You are not defined by how the world perceives you, but by how you recognize and utilize your unique talents.

Your abilities are your currency in the world. The more aware you are of what you bring to the table, the more empowered you will be to create opportunities, influence others, and live a life of purpose. The next step is putting these abilities into action, whether through career advancement, personal growth, or building powerful relationships.

Take time to reflect, assess, and embody your abilities. Your power starts with you, and the world is waiting for you to step into action.

Exercise: Self-Assessment Inventory

To get a clearer picture of your abilities, take a moment to reflect on the following questions:

- What activities make you feel energized and engaged?
- What do others frequently compliment you on?
- When do you feel most confident in your abilities?
- What problems do people often come to you for help with?
- If you had to teach a subject or skill, what would it be?

Recording your responses can help you identify patterns and recognize abilities you may have taken for granted.

Below are *my* Power Assets. I hope they help you reflect and identify yours, so you can see the result of this life-changing process.

My Assets:

1. Personal Strengths
- **Emotional Intelligence**—Deeply understands emotions and uses this to guide employees and coach clients effectively
- **Resilience**—Overcomes obstacles and helps others navigate challenges with mastery
- **Confidence**—Shows self-assurance through life situations, training, coaching, writing, and speaking
- **Willpower and Inner Strength**—Contains innate willpower to push past barriers and take control of life, and coach others to do so
- **Fluidity**—Changes directions and pivots quickly, not afraid of change, challenge, or conflict
- **Creativity**—Thinks outside the box and likes to create fun experiences
- **Nurturing and Feminine**—Uses feminine attributes to consciously nurture
- **Relatability**—Understands, relates, and talks to multiple types of people

2. Intellectual and Strategic Skills
- **Creative Problem-Solving**—Able to simplify complex problems for myself and others
- **Strategic Thinking**—Able to scale businesses to six, seven, and eight figures
- **Business Acumen**—Able to integrate nontraditional strategies with proven business models

- **Critical Thinking**—Able to blend mindset, business, and personal transformation to create unique success plans and teach them to others

3. Communication and Influence
- **Charisma and Presence**—Naturally attracts and inspires those seeking transformation
- **Articulation and Eloquence**—Speaks and delivers impactful coaching and workshops, three-time best-selling author, and magazine and newspaper contributor
- **Persuasion and Influence**—Helps others shift perspectives to transform their personal and professional lives
- **Likeability and Connection**—Builds strong friendships, networks, and deep relationships with employees and clients, earning their trust and loyalty

4. Productivity and Personal Effectiveness
- **Time Management Skills**—Balances multiple high-value services while scaling impact
- **Personal Style and Brand Presence**—Embodies the lifestyle and success that attracts friends, coaches, and ideal clients.
- **Resilient Work Ethic**—Demonstrates longevity, running very profitable businesses for decades, consistently showing up for work and life situations, and guides others through personal and professional growth

Bonus Assets:
- **Life Experience**—I deeply understand the transition from corporate to entrepreneurship.
- **Coaching Expertise**—I am a transformational coach, making profound shifts for my clients.
- **Visionary Leadership**—I help build businesses and design fulfilling lifestyles

- **Spiritual Articulation**—I am deeply empathic and gifted with profound intuitive abilities, holding a strong and unwavering connection to my Source. From this sacred alignment flows a powerful presence and clarity that guides and empowers both me and those I serve.

Reflections for You

1. **Confidence:** Where in your life have you stepped forward without all the answers and succeeded anyway? How did it feel?
2. **Resilience:** What challenge tested you the most, and what inner strength did you discover in the process?
3. **Self-Awareness:** What emotions or patterns do you notice in yourself when you are under pressure? How might you shift them toward alignment?
4. **Autonomy:** What area of your life currently feels out of your control, and how does reclaiming your personal power shift that dynamic?

Unlocking Your Personal Power: Self-Assessment

This self-assessment helps you measure your current sources of personal power and identify areas for growth.

Rate yourself from **1 (Needs Work)** to **5 (Strong Asset)**. Use the notes section for reflections or action ideas.

1. **Assets** (Qualities and Virtues You Can Leverage)
   Personal Strengths
   - Physical and emotional health: ___________
   - Confidence: ___________
   - Willpower and inner strength: ___________
   - Resilience: ___________

   Intellectual and Strategic Skills
   - Intelligence and reasoning: ___________

- Conflict management: ___________
- Creativity: ___________
- Strategy: ___________

Communication and Influence
- Communication: ___________
- Articulation: ___________
- Eloquence: ___________
- Likeability: ___________
- Personal presence: ___________
- Charm: ___________

Productivity and Personal Effectiveness
- Time management: ___________
- Life experience: ___________
- Personal style: ___________

Notes:

____
____
____
____
____
____
____
____
____
____

2. Abilities (Skills That Enhance Personal Power)
Self-Mastery and Decision-Making
- Willpower and discipline: ___________
- Decisiveness: ___________
- Emotional intelligence: ___________

- Adaptability: __________

Influence and Leadership
- Charisma: __________
- Public speaking: __________
- Persuasion and negotiation: __________
- Relationship-building: __________

Problem-Solving and Strategy
- Critical thinking: __________
- Conflict resolution: __________
- Risk assessment: __________
- Strategic planning: __________

Execution and Productivity
- Focus and prioritization: __________
- Time management: __________
- Goal setting and achievement: __________
- Resilience under pressure: __________

Now, highlight the abilities in each category with the highest score. These are your main assets. Use a different color to highlight the abilities with the lower scores that you want to work on, and put those aside for chapter 2 (*turning your imperfections into power*).

Reflection:

Which ability currently gives you the greatest edge?
What skill could elevate your leadership or business impact the most?

Notes:

____

____

____

____

____

____

____

____

Closing Reflection: The Courage to Stand Fully in Your Power

"The world doesn't need another imitation; it needs the fully expressed version of you."
~ Theresa Ream

Standing in your power is not about perfection or performance; it's about presence. It's the quiet, unshakable knowing that *your unique gifts are powerful* and that your unique mix of gifts, lessons, and life experiences wasn't random. They were the exact ingredients needed for the woman you were born to become.

When you finally stop waiting for permission, validation, or the "right moment," your life begins to shift. True power doesn't shout; it radiates. It's the calm confidence of a woman who knows who she is and why she's here.

Standing in your power means honoring your story, your scars, and your strengths. It means showing up authentically, even when your voice shakes. It means trusting that your intuition knows the way, even when logic doubts it.

Every ability you've cultivated, every hardship you've survived, and every dream that still stirs within you is part of your personal power portfolio. When you own it, you become magnetic. Opportunities find you. Relationships deepen, and your influence expands.

You don't have to chase power.

You *embody* it.

And when you do, you give others permission to do the same.

So today, take one small step that honors your abilities: speak up, create something, share your vision, or simply stand taller.

Because when you stand in your feminine power, the world shifts to meet you.

Action Plan: Living the Law of Standing in Your Power

1. Reclaim the Inner Ground of Power

Standing in your power begins with a simple yet profound shift in awareness. It is the moment you recognize that what you have been searching for outside of yourself has been within you all along. Power does not arrive later, after you achieve more, fix more, or become someone else. It is already present, woven through your experiences, your choices, and the way you have navigated your life.

Every skill you have developed, every insight you have gained, and every challenge you have endured have quietly shaped you for this moment. Even the experiences that felt messy, uncertain, or painful carried lessons that strengthened your intuition, resilience, and inner authority. When you begin to see your life through this lens, your story shifts from one effort to one preparation.

This week, create a sacred space to reconnect with what already makes you powerful. This is not a task to rush through or overanalyze. It is an invitation to slow down and listen to yourself with honesty and compassion. Find quiet moments where you can sit without distraction. Really take time, put it on your calendar. It's a process that should be taken seriously.

Take a breath. Let your body settle. Then, gently ask yourself the following questions:

Where in my life have I already been powerful, even if I did not recognize it at the time? Consider moments when you stood your ground, made a difficult decision, or moved forward despite fear. Power often shows up quietly in moments of endurance, clarity, or inner resolve.

What situations have revealed my courage, creativity, or intuition? Think about times when you trusted yourself, solved a problem in your own way, or sensed the right path before logic confirmed it. These moments are evidence of your innate wisdom.

What compliments or acknowledgments have I brushed aside that point to my strengths? Many women minimize praise, deflecting it out of habit or humility. Revisit the words others have offered you and allow yourself to receive them fully. Often, they reflect qualities you have yet to fully claim.

As you answer these questions, write everything down. Do not edit yourself. Do not judge what appears. The act of naming your power anchors it into truth. It transforms vague awareness into something solid and tangible. When you write it, you begin to recognize it and own it.

This process is not about ego or comparison. It is about remembering. It is about returning to yourself and recognizing the strength that has always been there, steady and present, even when you doubted it. When you reclaim the inner ground of power, you stop looking outward for permission or validation. You begin to trust your own voice, your own timing, and your own way of leading.

Standing in your power is not a destination. It is a daily relationship with yourself. And it begins here, by acknowledging what has already been true about you all along.

Affirmation: I stand rooted in the truth of who I am. My power is not something to prove; it is something to remember not only in my mind but in my body.

2. Identify and Honor Your Core Abilities

Remember, your abilities are your energetic currency. To stand in your power, you must know the tools you carry. Revisit your chapter inventory and choose three core abilities that define you most right now. They might be emotional intelligence, resilience, creativity, leadership, or intuitive insight.

For each of your abilities you scored high on, answer the following questions below:

- How have I used this ability to create change or impact?
- Can I monetize this ability?
- How could I expand or express it more fully in my business, relationships, or purpose?

When you understand your gifts, you can leverage them intentionally instead of unconsciously. Many women undervalue what comes naturally, believing ease equals insignificance. But the truth is the opposite: what comes naturally is your genius zone.

Affirmation: My natural gifts are divine assignments. What flows easily from me is meant to flow through me.

3. Transform Abilities into Assets

Abilities become powerful only when applied. Turning them into assets means aligning them with purpose and vision.

For each of your three core abilities, create an action statement. Here are a few examples:

- "I will use my creativity to design workshops that empower women to find their voice."
- "I will use my empathy to strengthen team culture and resolve conflict gracefully."
- "I will use my strategic mind to build scalable systems that support freedom."

Then, put these abilities into motion this month. Choose one specific project, collaboration, or conversation where you can express these gifts boldly. Action activates potential, building momentum and confidence.

If you find yourself waiting for the "perfect" moment, remember: Confidence comes through motion, not before it. Expecting to attain confidence without action is putting the cart before the horse. Confidence is *earned* when we feel fear and do it anyway, even if we are bad at it the first few times. The biggest mistake is thinking we need confidence before acting. Without action, true confidence will remain elusive.

Affirmation: My abilities expand through action. Every step I take strengthens my power.

4. Release Comparison and Reclaim Authentic Expression

You cannot stand in your power if you are standing in someone else's shadow. Comparison dilutes your energy. Authenticity magnifies it.

Every time you catch yourself thinking, *she's more successful, more confident, more advanced than I am,* hit pause. Then reframe:

She is simply a mirror of what's possible for me.

Notice how your energy shifts from contraction to expansion.

This week, do something that expresses *you,* your voice, your perspective, your style. Write that post in your own tone, not the industry trend. Wear what makes you feel radiant, not what you think you "should." Say the thing you've been censoring.

The feminine path to power is expression, not perfection. Your authenticity is the bridge to every opportunity meant for you.

Affirmation: I no longer shrink to fit spaces I've outgrown. My authenticity is my magnetism.

5. Strengthen Your Relationships as Power Sources

In the feminine model of leadership, relationships are not distractions; they are the conduits of influence.

Look around you. Who are the people that light you up, challenge you, and call you higher? Who believes in you when you forget to believe in yourself? These are your allies. And equally important: Where are you leaking energy by over-giving, rescuing, or seeking approval? Those dynamics quietly drain your power.

Take inventory this week:

- Who are my energetic allies?
- Who needs clearer boundaries?
- Where can I show up more authentically in my connections?

Reach out to one person who embodies mutual growth and share your gratitude for them. Then lovingly distance yourself from any relationship that keeps you in smallness or self-doubt. We will discuss this in-depth later in the book.

Affirmation: I attract relationships rooted in mutual respect, trust, and expansion.

6. Lead with Grace and Decisiveness

Standing in power requires courage to decide. The feminine leader doesn't force outcomes; she directs energy with clarity. Each decision, big or small, is an act of self-trust.

If indecision has kept you stagnant, practice making intuitive micro-decisions daily.

Ask yourself:

- What feels most aligned right now?

- What would I choose if I already believed in my success and trusted my power?

Make the choice; then move. *Clarity comes from more commitment and action and a little less contemplation.*

If a decision feels overwhelming, zoom out. Ask yourself, *What's the most loving choice for my highest self and everyone involved right now?* That one question will rarely lead you astray and help you move quickly through a decision-making process. You can always correct the course during the process. Nothing is set in stone, and you have the right to change your mind and direction as needed.

Affirmation: I trust myself to make aligned decisions. Every choice I make strengthens who I am meant to become.

7. Build Power Through Embodiment

Feminine Power is not a mindset; it's a practice of embodiment. The way you walk, speak, breathe, and hold yourself sends energetic signals before a word is spoken. To embody your power:

- Stand tall with your shoulders open and head lifted
- Speak slowly and clearly, allowing silence to punctuate your authority
- Enter rooms with intention, not apology

Every time you embody your feminine power, you train your nervous system to believe it. Over time, your power stops being a costume and becomes your skin. Remember, others read our bodies with their bodies. As humans, we also have animal bodies that pick up signals from both other humans and animals. Align your mind with your body so others feel your authenticity.

You might even create a Power Ritual before key meetings, networking, or workshops—ground your energy, breathe deeply, and affirm.

Affirmation: My presence and body speak before I do. I am calm, powerful, and magnetic. I am a vessel of clarity, wisdom, and grace. I do not perform power; I radiate it.

8. Turn Reflection into Ritual

Awareness without reflection fades; reflection without action stagnates. Combine both to create transformation.

Every Sunday evening, or whenever works for you, schedule twenty minutes for your Power Reflection Ritual.

Ask yourself:

1. What abilities did I express this week?
2. What moments made me feel most powerful?
3. Where did I give away my energy, and what boundary can I reinforce?
4. How can I lead with more authenticity next week?
5. Have I practiced embodying my power so I give strong signals for others to pick up?

Create and document your insights in a Power Journal. Over time, you'll see patterns emerging—a visible map of your evolution. You'll also notice that standing in your power is not an act of courage, but a way of life.

Affirmation: I evolve with intention. Each reflection propels me into mastery.

9. Anchor Your Vision of Empowered Living

Now that you've identified your abilities and begun to align your actions, anchor your vision. Close your eyes and imagine your life one year from now when you are fully standing in your power. Vision boarding is a great exercise. Every vision board I created began decades ago and now stands as a testament to my life and the visions that I have set to realize. I would say at least ninety percent of what I put on my vision boards came to be.

Get specific on your visions:

- What do you envision your business and lifestyle to look like?
- How do you speak, move, and create?
- Who surrounds you?
- What impact are you making?
- How would you like to appear?

Visualize it vividly. Let it move from imagination into embodiment. Then, write a declaration in your journal beginning with, "I am the woman who …"
Examples:

- *I am the woman who leads with grace and authority.*
- *I am the woman whose words inspire action.*
- *I am the woman who knows her worth and walks in it with confidence.*

Read your declaration aloud daily. Speak it until it becomes your reality.

Affirmation: I no longer wait for permission to stand in my power. I am already everything I was born to be.

10. Commit to Consistent Action

Power grows through consistency. Choose one tangible commitment to practice over the next thirty days:

- Launch that offering
- Speak on that stage

- Reach out to that collaborator and build something together
- Say "no" where you've been saying "yes" out of obligation
- Say "yes" to something you've been saying "no" to out of fear

Track your actions each week and celebrate every courageous step. Remember, feminine power isn't measured by how fast you move; it's measured by walking in alignment.

Affirmation: I am consistent in my courage. Every action I take affirms my worth and the worth of those around me.

Standing in your power isn't a one-time revelation; it's a daily recalibration. It's remembering that your worth is not conditional, your power is not borrowed, and your gifts are not accidental.

Each time you choose authenticity over approval, courage over comfort, and alignment over fear, you strengthen the foundation of your feminine power.

"The world doesn't need a smaller version of you. It needs the woman who knows her value, embodies her vision, and leads with heart."
~ Theresa Ream

Final Affirmation: I am the embodiment of power, purpose, and grace. I no longer chase power; I am it.

Chapter Two: The Law of Turning Your Imperfections into Power

"Grace is what holds the stars and planets in place. Our entire beings are floating in an invisible universe of grace."
~ Theresa Ream

Power isn't the absence of flaws; it's the mastery of them. You were born powerful, even with your mess, your fears, your shadows, and your contradictions.

For years, I thought my imperfections were proof that I wasn't enough. My lack of consistency. My restlessness. My jumping from one thing to another. My tendency to over-commit. To avoid what I didn't like or thought I wasn't good at. To grip too tightly at the wheel, instead of delegating. My fear of looking foolish. My resistance to asking for help, even when I knew I needed it.

I carried those patterns like secret sins, convinced they disqualified me from the kind of power I admired in others. But here's the truth no one tells you—Your shadows are not the end of your story; they are the birthplace of your strategy, your creativity, and your resilience.

And I am not alone. Every woman I've coached has her own list. And when she finally lays it bare, she always believes she's the only one. Until she sees others' lists. Until she hears another woman say the exact same words. Then, suddenly, she realizes: *It's not just me.*

The moment you stop hiding your imperfections is the moment you begin to reclaim your power. Because what you once saw as weakness can become your edge. My restlessness became a gift of reinvention. My inconsistency taught me to create systems and connect with allies to support me where I wavered. My over-commitment showed me the art of boundaries. And my fear of looking foolish pushed me into courage, into speaking when my voice shook, into raising my hand when I was trembling.

> "Not all 'flaws' need to be fixed. Most just need to be understood."
> ~ *Theresa Ream*

The following are the patterns I see frequently in myself and in my clients:

- Lack of consistency on projects due to over-commitment
- Restlessness and jumping from one thing to another
- Not breaking things down to their simplest form
- Multi-tasking and lack of focus
- Controlling situations and not delegating
- Avoiding tasks they don't like instead of delegating
- Letting fear stop them and not pushing through
- Fear of looking bad or "stupid"
- Not using their connections for growth and help as much as they should
- Not asking for help as much as they should

Sound familiar? *These aren't quirks; they're patterns that echo across women who are visionaries, builders, mothers, leaders, and creators.*

When you see these "shortcomings" for what they are, not shameful flaws but signals of your deeper strengths, you can begin to alchemize them. Over-commitment is the flip side of vision; it means your dreams are abundant, not scarce. Restlessness is the heartbeat of innovation; it keeps you from settling on mediocrity. The need to control is rooted in devotion; you care so much about the outcome that you forget others may have gifts to contribute too. Even avoidance is wisdom in disguise; it shows you where your energy is not meant to flow, reminding you to honor your zone of genius.

Your shadows don't disqualify you; they are the compass, pointing toward your next level of leadership. When you recognize them with compassion, you gain the freedom to transform them into strategies, partnerships, and practices that support the woman you are becoming.

Here's the secret: Your "mess" is the raw material for your message. The cracks are not something to patch over; they are the places where your light seeps out. Think of a woman you admire most deeply. Is she perfect? No. What makes her unforgettable is the way she owns her scars, the way she walks into the room with both strength and softness, the way she makes you feel less alone in your humanity.

When we permit ourselves to lead from our wholeness, the polished and the raw, we free other women to do the same. Power is contagious when it is honest. And there is nothing more magnetic than a woman who is boldly herself, flaws and all.

So instead of striving to "fix" what you think is wrong with you, start asking: How can I turn this into fuel? How can I shape this into a strategy? How can this imperfection become the very way I inspire and influence others?

Because here's the truth: Your power was never meant to be flawless. It was meant to be real. It's meant to be leveraged to our highest potential.

The first step is radical honesty. Power grows in the light, not in the shadows of "I'll do better tomorrow." I had to admit truths about myself, not as flaws to be hidden, but as patterns waiting to be alchemized, such as:

- I overcommit because I am lit with vision, sometimes too big for one lifetime.
- I leap from one thing to another because my creativity outruns my discipline.
- I try to control things because I care deeply about the outcome and am devoted to excellence.
- My avoidance may be intuition saying: *This was never yours to carry.*
- I fear looking foolish because I've built empires from scratch, and I want them to endure. (And doesn't fear whisper at the door of every woman who dares to lead?)
- I question if I resist asking for help because I hold the conviction of an outcome that's truly mine.

These confessions are not weaknesses; they are the raw materials of strength. Once named, they lose their power to shame us and instead become the very places where wisdom, strategy, and feminine leadership are born. You see, there is power inside your shortcomings.

Do you see the thread? Every "shortcoming" is tethered to strength.

What we call flaws are, in truth, strengths stretched beyond balance.

When you start to see your shortcomings through this lens, you realize they were never meant to be chains; they were always clues. Over-commitment, for instance, isn't proof of failure; it's a reminder to refine your focus so your vision doesn't scatter, but sharpens. Restlessness isn't a curse; it is the invitation to pioneer, to bring forth new ideas before the world even knows it needs them. Control, when softened, becomes stewardship: Your fierce love for outcomes channeled into guiding others to rise with you.

Even fear, the companion we so often despise, is a teacher. It signals that you're standing at the threshold of expansion. Fear only knocks when you're about to cross into something greater. And avoidance? It's the soul's way of whispering: *Not here. Not this. Redirect.*

What if you could begin treating each so-called weakness as an oracle? Instead of shame, you'd find strategy. Instead of exhaustion, you'd find clarity. This is the alchemy of feminine power: turning what the world calls weakness into wisdom.

Your power does not come from erasing your imperfections, but from standing tall with them, reshaped, reframed, and reclaimed as the hidden strengths they always were.

Rising Above

"Delegation isn't surrender; it's expansion. Every time you let go, your empire grows."
~ Theresa Ream

Here's what I know now: my flaws were never liabilities; they were raw material.

- Over-commitment forged my discernment
- Restlessness sharpened my innovation
- Avoidance reminded me that I don't have to do everything myself and to examine what I truly want
- Fear carved out my courage
- Not asking for help revealed the truth—allies are not optional; they are essential

And I've watched the same transformation in my clients. The moment they stop judging their flaws and start designing power through them, everything changes.

If I had waited until I was "fixed," you would not be holding this book. **My power came because I danced with my limitations, not because I erased them.**

A Client Story: How Kris Reframed Shame into Strength

Kris sat across from me. She spoke softly, as if her shortcomings might hear her and rise in protest. On the surface, she was accomplished. She was smart, capable, and deeply respected in her field. But beneath that competence lived a quiet, constant shame. She believed something was fundamentally wrong with her. She felt too sensitive, easily affected by a person's tone, mood, or unspoken tension in a room. She hesitated before speaking or deciding, second-guessing her timing and instincts. She had a habit of minimizing herself, softening her opinions and achievements so she would not take up too much space. She carried an unspoken responsibility for other people's emotions, often adjusting herself to keep others comfortable. And beneath it all was a persistent self-doubt, a fear that if she were fully seen, she would be exposed as not enough, flawed, or even weird.

For years, Kris carried these patterns like evidence against herself. She believed they disqualified her from leadership, from visibility, from real power. Every self-doubt became proof of failure. Every moment of hesitation reinforced the story that she was not enough.

The first step was not fixing anything; it was naming.

In our early sessions, I asked her to write down every trait she felt ashamed of. She hesitated, then finally filled the page. When she finished, she stared at it, waiting for judgment.

Instead, I asked her a different question. "What if none of this is a flaw?"

That question cracked something open.

Reframing Moment

The reframing came next. We stopped treating her sensitivity as something to toughen up and began honoring it as perception. What she had labeled hesitation revealed itself as discernment, a natural pause that allowed her to sense timing, alignment, and truth. Her habit of minimizing herself was no longer seen as a lack of confidence but as an old strategy for staying safe in spaces that were not built to hold her fullness. Taking responsibility for other people's emotions was not weakness but empathy without boundaries, a strength that had never been taught where or when to stop. Even her self-doubt shifted meaning. It was not proof of incompetence but evidence of care, integrity, and a deep desire to do things well. When these qualities were seen clearly, they no longer required fixing. They required direction, protection, and permission to mature into leadership.

For the first time, Kris felt relief. Not because she was excused, but because she was understood, which was the beginning of truly understanding herself.

Reframing is the conscious act of changing the meaning we assign to our traits, patterns, and experiences so they can be seen in their true light. It is not about denying reality or pretending challenges do not exist, but about interpreting them through a lens of wisdom instead of judgment. Through reframing, what once appeared as weakness is revealed as undeveloped strength. What was labeled as a flaw becomes information. It allows a woman to release shame and recognize that many of her most criticized qualities were adaptations, formed in environments that did not know how to receive her depth. Reframing restores self-trust by replacing self-criticism with understanding. When meaning changes, identity changes, and when identity changes, power becomes available.

Reframing is powerful because it changes the story you are living inside. Long before a woman changes her behavior, her strategy, or her circumstances, she must change the meaning she has assigned to herself. Our interpretation of a meaning shapes our identity, and identity shapes every choice that follows. When a woman believes something about herself is a flaw, she will manage, hide, or fight it. When that same trait is understood as a strength waiting for guidance, she begins to lead with it. Reframing opens the door to self-respect and self-trust. It releases energy that was once trapped in self-protection and makes it available for creativity, confidence, and leadership. Nothing about the woman changes in that moment, yet everything does.

Reframing shifts everything. Instead of punishing yourself for these tendencies, start asking: *What truth does this reveal about me? What strength is hiding inside this shadow?* That's where power is born. When women gather and speak these truths, we realize we are not broken; we are brilliant. We are not failing; we are evolving.

The third step in working with Kris was designing support instead of demanding perfection. Rather than trying to discipline herself into someone she was not, she began shaping her life around how she functions best. She simplified decisions that once drained her energy. She created gentle anchors in her week that kept her grounded when her emotions ran high. She stopped expecting herself to remember everything and built reminders, checklists, and rhythms that held her steady. She gave herself permission to rest before she was depleted and to ask for support before she was overwhelmed. With each small adjustment, the pressure eased. The chaos did not disappear overnight, but it no longer ruled her. Structure became a form of self-respect and support replaced self-criticism.

Then came her most vulnerable step. Visibility.

Kris had spent years hiding her voice, convinced she would sound unpolished or say the wrong thing. We worked on letting her speak anyway. First, in small rooms. Then, in group settings. Her voice shook. She did it anyway. And something unexpected happened. People leaned in. They trusted her more, not less.

What she feared would expose her connected her.

The shame that once ruled her began to loosen its grip. She no longer whispered her imperfections as confessions. She spoke of them as context. As experience. As wisdom earned.

Months later, Kris said something I will never forget.

"I used to think my flaws were the reason I couldn't lead. Now I see they are the reason people listen and follow; they want a leader that is real."

Her power did not come from becoming flawless. It came from becoming whole.

She stopped hiding the parts she once believed were unacceptable. In doing so, she gave other women permission to do the same. Her leadership became warmer. Her presence more magnetic. Her confidence no longer brittle but grounded.

Kris did not erase her shortcomings. She mastered them by working with them. She learned that power does not require perfection. It requires honesty, compassion, and courage to stop pretending and to walk through fear to get to the other side.

And that is the moment shame turns into strength. Not when you finally get it right, but when you finally stop believing you are wrong.

Four Steps to Overcoming Shame

Shame rarely begins with us. It is often inherited, absorbed through family systems, cultural expectations, and unspoken rules about who we are allowed to be. Many women were raised in environments where success was downplayed, emotions were dismissed, mistakes were punished, or visibility was dangerous. Over time, these messages harden into a collective internal voice that says: don't stand out, don't ask for more, don't get it wrong.

But inherited shame is not destiny; it is a pattern. And patterns can be interrupted.

Step 1: Name the Inherited Shame

Shame thrives in secrecy. The first act of power is recognition.

Begin by asking: *Whose voice does this sound like?*

Is the shame tied to family messages, such as:

- "Don't get too big for your britches."
- "Who do you think you are?"
- "We don't do things like that."
- "Better to be safe than sorry.
- "Who asked for your opinion?"

When you trace shame back to its origin, it often reveals itself as protection, not truth. It was passed down to survive, fit in, or avoid risk. Naming it breaks the illusion that it belongs to you.

Say this out loud: "This shame did not begin with me."

Awareness creates distance. Distance creates choices.

Step 2: Separate Shame from Identity

Shame convinces you that *you are* the problem, not that you experienced one.

This step is about dismantling that lie.

Instead of saying, "I am inconsistent," shift to, "I have a pattern of inconsistency."

Instead of, "I'm too much," say, "I learned to dim myself to belong."

This subtle shift separates behavior from worth. It returns your identity to its rightful place as whole and intact.

Family shame often confuses love with compliance. But your worth was never dependent on behaving correctly, staying small, or carrying the emotional weight of others. You are not responsible for maintaining old family roles at the expense of your truth.

You are allowed to evolve and grow into your full power.

Step 3: Reframe the Shadow as Survival Wisdom

Every shame pattern once served a purpose.

What looks like a flaw today was often a survival strategy in the past.

- Staying quiet kept you safe
- Over-functioning earned love
- Perfection prevented criticism
- Avoidance protected you from failure

When you honor the original intention, shame softens. You stop fighting yourself and start listening.

Ask yourself:

What was this pattern trying to protect me from? What strength developed because of it?

Reframing transforms shame into self-respect. You realize you were not weak; you were adaptive. And now, as an adult woman with agency, you get to choose new ways to meet your needs without self-betrayal.

Stop asking, *how do I erase this flaw?* And start asking, *how do I design power around it?*

For example:

- The woman who over-commits learns to guard her *yeses* like diamonds.
- The restless creator keeps a notebook to park ideas, so she doesn't abandon the project in front of her.
- The multi-tasker trains herself in single-tasking bursts that move mountains.
- The controller practices delegation as an act of trust, not surrender.

- The one afraid of looking foolish learns to feel the fear and move anyway, because power never waits for permission.
- The woman who never asks for help discovers that asking is not weakness; it is weaving allies into the fabric of her empire.

Delegation is no longer weakness; it is legacy. Every time you hand off something to someone else, you expand the kingdom of feminine power instead of shrinking it to your own two hands.

Your shortcomings are not your shame. They are your secret strategy.

Stop running from them. Dance with them. Work with them. Rise above them.

Because the woman who owns her shortcomings and fears without apology is unstoppable.

"You were not born to be flawless. You were born powerful, and power is forged in the raw, unpolished, imperfect edges of your life."
~ Theresa Ream

Step 4: Break the Cycle through Compassionate Boundaries

Shame ends when the pattern ends.

This step requires courage and consistency.

You break family shame by refusing to participate in conversations, dynamics, or expectations that reinforce it. That may mean:

- Not explaining or defending your choices
- Choosing visibility even when it makes others uncomfortable

- Saying no without apology or explaining
- Allowing others to feel disappointed without rescuing them

Compassion does not mean compliance.

You can love your family and still choose differently. You can honor your roots without living in their limitations.

Each time you respond from self-trust instead of shame, you rewrite the legacy, not just for yourself, but for everyone who comes after you.

Realizing the Truth

Shame is not proof that something is wrong with you; it is proof that you are standing at the edge of change.

When you name it, separate it, reframe it, and set boundaries around it, shame loses its power. What remains is clarity, self-respect, and a deeper connection to who you truly are.

You are not here to carry what was never yours.

You are here to transform yourself and others into the powerful beings God intended. Because that is feminine power in its most courageous form.

Reflection

Take inventory. Not of your glossy strengths, but of the places you hide.

Where do you scatter instead of focus?

Where do you control instead of trust?

Where does fear grip you at the throat?

Now look again. What gift is hiding inside that shortcoming? What system, ally, or boundary could turn it into fuel?

This practice is not about judgment; it is about reclamation. When you write down the places you feel small, scattered, or afraid, you are not confessing sins; you are uncovering hidden treasure. Every woman I've coached who has dared to be this honest discovers the same thing: The very place she feels most inadequate is the doorway to her next level of power. Your restlessness may be asking you to innovate. Your tendency to control may be begging you to delegate and create space for others to shine. Your fear of being seen may be nudging you to finally step onto the stage where your voice can shift the atmosphere. None of this is about fixing yourself; it is about partnering with your truth, redirecting it with grace, and allowing it to serve you instead of sabotage you. So, as you take this inventory, sit with each shortcoming until you hear its whisper: *I am not here to break you. I am here to grow you.* Real power comes when you no longer waste energy running from your shadows. Instead, you claim them, honor them, and then use them to light the way forward.

Overcoming Self-Doubt and Recognizing Your Worth

"The moment you stop hiding from your weaknesses, they stop running your life."
~ Theresa Ream

In working with leadership teams, I have found that self-doubt is a huge common denominator. Many struggle with self-doubt, minimizing their abilities or feeling like they are not "good enough." This mindset can be one of the biggest barriers to success. Recognizing and owning your abilities requires shifting your internal dialogue from self-criticism to self-empowerment.

Strategies to Overcome Self-Doubt

1. **Acknowledge Your Wins:** Keep a journal of accomplishments, no matter how small. Seeing your progress over time reinforces your confidence.

2. **Seek Feedback:** Ask trusted mentors, friends, or colleagues what they see as your strengths. Sometimes, others recognize our abilities before we do. I know from experience that my greatest mentors saw my abilities before I did.

3. **Challenge Negative Thoughts:** Ask, when you doubt yourself, *What evidence do I have that I am incapable?* Often, fear is unfounded.

4. **Keep a list of your abilities:** Refer to it often. Knowing and walking in your strengths will do wonders for keeping self-doubt at bay.

Surround Yourself with Supportive People

Being around those who uplift and challenge you will help you recognize and develop your abilities. For me, that support has come most powerfully from the circle of business girlfriends I travel with and connect with through networking groups. These women aren't just colleagues; they are allies who see me, remind me of my brilliance when I forget, and hold me accountable to the vision I carry. When we gather at retreats, conferences, or even casual trips together, the conversations are rich with strategy, encouragement, and laughter. We swap stories of both triumphs and failures, and in doing so, we normalize the truth that no one does this journey alone. Their support feels like a net beneath me when I leap and a mirror in front of me when I need to remember who I am. Surrounding myself with women who walk with courage and vulnerability has been one of the most powerful choices I've made for my growth as a leader.

How My Moment of Fear Turned to Pride and Confidence

"Fear will always knock, but with practice, power answers first." ~ Theresa Ream

I'll never forget the night on the mastermind cruise when courage found me in the most unexpected way. After a long day of learning and laughter, the evening turned playful, and ten of my business girlfriends were lined up to do stand-up comedy. One after another, they took the mic, bold and brilliant, turning their stories into humor that lit up the room. I sat in the audience, heart pounding, watching them shine.

And then a voice rose up inside me: *I can do that!*

It terrified me. My hands shook, my throat tightened, but I knew this was a moment I couldn't ignore. I walked straight over to Caterina, the organizer, and whispered through my fear, "I want to go next." She smiled and nodded with approval, and just like that, I was on stage: raw, unprepared, and completely alive.

To my surprise, I did well. The room erupted in laughter, and in that instant, I felt a surge of confidence ripple through me. Even now, women from that cruise still mention my performance, reminding me that courage isn't about being fearless, it's about being willing.

That night taught me something essential: The very imperfections I thought disqualified me, like my fear of looking foolish and a lingering undercurrent that I wasn't good enough, were the birthplace of my power. What I once labeled as weakness became the very qualities that made me magnetic, relatable, and brave. This is the alchemy of feminine power: turning our flaws into fire.

Identifying Your Shortcomings and Shadows

"You were born powerful. Your flaws just remind you where your strength is still waiting to be claimed."
~ Theresa Ream

Purpose

Your "shortfalls" are not signs of weakness; they are invitations to refinement, clarity, and power.

This reflection helps you uncover where your energy leaks and where your hidden strengths lie.

Step 1: Honest Reflection

Check or note any of the patterns that feel familiar:

- ☐ I say yes too often and struggle to stay consistent.
- ☐ I start many things but finish few.
- ☐ I overthink or complicate what could be simple.
- ☐ I juggle too much and lose focus.
- ☐ I have a hard time delegating or trusting others to help.
- ☐ I avoid tasks I dislike instead of assigning or outsourcing them.
- ☐ I let fear of looking foolish stop me from taking bold action.
- ☐ I crave approval, validation, or recognition.
- ☐ I rarely ask for help, even when I need it.
- ☐ I'm harder on myself than anyone else ever could be.

Step 2: The Shadow Beneath the Strength

For each one you checked, complete these prompts:

1. This pattern shows up most often when I feel

____.

2. The strength underneath this liability might be
    ____.
3. When I fall into this pattern, it costs me
    ____.
    (time, peace, confidence, connection).
4. When I rise above it, I gain
    ____.

Step 3: Reclaiming Power

Reflect on the following:

1. What am I still trying to prove by carrying so much on my own?
2. Where in my life do I confuse control with care?
3. What fear keeps me from trusting others or myself?
4. What boundary, system, or ally could help me turn this liability into leverage?
5. If my shadow could speak, what truth would it want me to know right now?

Step 4: Power Reframe

Write a personal affirmation that transforms one of your flaws into a statement of strength.

Example:

"I am inconsistent," can become, "I am a visionary learning to focus my brilliance."

Now, write your own:

____

____

"The parts of you that you hide are often the parts carrying your greatest strength."
~ Theresa Ream

Action Plan: Turning Shadows into Power

1. Recognize the Shadow, Reclaim the Light

Power begins with awareness.

Before transformation comes recognition, the willingness to face what you've been hiding from. Make time each evening for an *honest inventory*. Ask yourself:

- Where did I self-sabotage today?
- When did fear or control take over?
- What was I protecting myself from?

Naming the shadow removes its ability to shame you. Write each "flaw" in a journal, and beside it, write the hidden intention or desire beneath it.

For example:

"My over-commitment comes from my deep desire to serve."

"My restlessness means I'm ready for new growth."

Awareness turns judgment into data. Every self-realized woman knows you cannot transform what you refuse to look at.

2. Reframe Each Shadow into a Strength

Every shadow carries a seed of brilliance. The next step is to reframe. For every pattern you identify, complete this sentence:

"The strength underneath this flaw is ______________."

Example reframes:

- Over-commitment → Visionary leadership and passion
- Restlessness → Innovation and adaptability
- Control → Devotion to excellence
- Avoidance → Intuitive redirection toward what matters most
- Fear → Indicator of growth and expansion

Keep this list visible. You are teaching your mind to recognize your own genius instead of criticizing your humanity. Reframing creates a new energetic blueprint, one of empowerment instead of resistance.

3. Design Systems that Support You

Once you know your tendencies, create *structures that serve your strengths*.

A good system is not rigid or punishing; it is compassionate structure. It exists to support who you are, not who you think you "should" be. A well-designed system anticipates your tendencies and holds you steady when your energy fluctuates. It removes decision fatigue, softens self-judgment, and replaces willpower with wisdom. For example, knowing my tendency to over-focus and then burn out, I built a rhythm that honors both productivity and embodiment: I work in focused, intentional blocks of no more than an hour. Then I get up and move my body, organize something physical, load the dishwasher, or do a few squats or pushups. This isn't procrastination; it's regulation. The system works because it meets me where I am. The same is true for delegation systems, visibility practices, or calendar boundaries. A powerful system thinks for you in moments when emotion, fear, or exhaustion might otherwise take the wheel. It quietly reinforces your boundaries, protects your energy, and keeps you aligned with your highest intentions. Systems, when designed with self-honor, become sacred containers that allow your brilliance to flow without collapse.

Consider the following:

- **If you over-commit**—Practice saying "let me check my calendar" before saying yes. Schedule creative time first and protect it fiercely.
- **If you avoid delegation**—Choose one task this week to entrust to someone else. Celebrate the act of releasing control as an act of leadership.
- **If you fear visibility**—Post, speak, or share something small but personal. Each act builds your courage muscle.

"Systems are sacred; they hold your power steady when emotion or exhaustion tries to derail you."
~ Theresa Ream

4. Build Your Circle of Grace

Grace is multiplied through connection. You cannot evolve in isolation. The feminine path to power is relational. Surround yourself with allies, women who mirror your brilliance, challenge your limits, and remind you of who you are when you forget.

Practice grace and learn to delegate. Each time you ask for help, you weave another thread in your empire's fabric. Delegation isn't surrender; it's expansion.

Create a support ritual

- Once a month, gather a few trusted peers to share one shadow you're working through and one strength that's emerging.
- Reflect to each other not the problem, but the *potential*.

5. Replace Criticism with Compassion

Every time self-judgment arises, meet it with compassion. Speak to yourself as you would to your closest friend:
It's OK to grow and learn.
I am growing through this, not failing because of it."
When your mind wants to punish you for being imperfect, pause. Place your hand over your heart and whisper:
I am in process. I am power in progress.
Compassion is not softness; it is the discipline of love. It keeps you from turning your power against yourself.

6. Take Bold, Imperfect Action

Perfectionism is the shadow's last defense. Break it by acting before you feel ready.

- Volunteer to lead a meeting
- Host a workshop or share your story
- Speak even when your voice shakes

Remember my cruise story, and the power of saying "yes" to courage? Action dissolves fear faster than overthinking ever will.

Each time you act through imperfection, you prove that your worth is not dependent on flawless performance. You expand your capacity to lead, inspire, and influence.

7. Journal into Power

Answer the following questions:

1. Which "flaw" do I avoid admitting, and what strength is buried inside it?
2. Where in my life am I over-carrying what was never mine?

3. Who could I trust with what drains me?
4. Where in my life am I still trying to prove I can "do it all alone"?
5. What would it look like to let my "weaknesses" be my teacher?

End each week with three journal prompts:

1. What shadow showed up most strongly this week, and what truth was it trying to reveal?
2. How did I turn one imperfection into a strength in action?
3. Where did I show courage instead of control?

This reflection practice turns self-awareness into transformation. Over time, you'll see that your greatest growth came not from your polished moments, but from the places you dared to face.

8. Anchor with a Power Reframe

Write an affirmation that transforms one flaw into light.
For example:
"I am not inconsistent; I am a visionary learning to channel my brilliance."
"I am not controlling; I am a leader practicing trust."
"I am not afraid; I am expanding into courage."
Repeat it daily. Your words are spells that reshape your self-image.

9. Embody the Lesson

Power is not theory; it's embodiment. Each time you choose self-honesty over shame, delegation over control, trust over fear, you are living the alchemy of feminine power.

You are showing other women that leadership does not require perfection; it requires presence.

10.   Remember the Core Truth

"Your shortcomings are not your shame; they are your secret strategy." ~ Theresa Ream

The real work is not to become flawless but *fully integrated.*
Your shadows are sacred teachers.
Your imperfections are invitations to mastery.
When you dance with them, you rise.
When you hide from them, you shrink.
So today, make the choice every powerful woman must make, to turn your shadows into strategy, your fear into faith, and your flaws into fire.

That is where true power begins, and where your legacy is born.

Chapter Three: The Law of Allies and Amplifiers

"You don't need a crowd. You need a circle that's invested in your rise." ~ Theresa Ream

Your allies and amplifiers are supportive people, mentors, collaborators, and relationships that multiply your influence. Power is never built in isolation. No matter how strong, wise, or independent you are, your personal power will always be influenced by the people around you. That's why one of your greatest assets isn't just your talents; it's your allies.

Allies aren't just cheerleaders clapping from the sidelines. They're collaborators, truth-tellers, door-openers, and protectors. They help you stand stronger, see further, and move faster. And when chosen and nurtured well, they become part of the very foundation of your power.

An ally is someone who supports your interests, contributes to your success, and most importantly, speaks for you when you're not in the room. An ally propels you forward and uplifts you.

But let's be real, most relationships are conditional. That's not bad; it's human. People help others based on shared values, mutual respect, emotional bonds, or aligned self-interest. Understanding this allows you to form alliances with eyes wide open.

Building powerful alliances isn't manipulating; it's about mutual empowerment.

Allies are often forged around:

- Shared values
- Shared experiences

- Shared enemies or obstacles
- Mutual admiration and respect

I wasn't always good at leaning on allies. In the early years of running my business, I thought being a strong leader meant carrying everything myself. I pushed through long hours, took on too many roles, and convinced myself I didn't need help. But when we faced a tough season—financial strain, staff turnover, and major projects colliding—I realized I couldn't do it alone. That was the turning point. My allies showed up: trusted team members, mentors, coaches, and even other business owners who had walked the road before me. They steadied the ground under my feet when it felt like it was giving way. Since then, I've never forgotten the power of having the right people around me.

One of my first experiences with true allyship came when I joined a professional women's network many years ago. I knew no one, felt completely out of place, and certainly didn't see myself as a seasoned businesswoman. But Sandra, a woman who carried herself with ease and confidence, saw something in me that I hadn't yet recognized. She treated me as if I belonged there, as if I was already capable and wonderful. She took me under her wing, introduced me to others, and gave me the confidence to step into a role I didn't even know I was ready for. Her belief in me helped shape the businesswoman I am today. That's the quiet but profound power of an ally; they see your potential before you do, and they lend you their strength until you can stand in your own. I later became president of that organization many times throughout the years. I never would have dreamed that was possible, walking into that first meeting.

You see this same principle play out everywhere, even in Hollywood. Think of how certain actors and directors like Adam Sandler always work together with the same actors for decades, movie after movie. It's fun to watch; you can tell they are great friends, because they know they can count on one another's strengths. It's not just friendship; it's allyship. And whether you're building a business, stepping into a new community, or making a movie, allies are the hidden force behind lasting success.

You Only Need a Few Key Allies

"Allyship isn't about networking; it's about devotion. Give it. Receive it. Honor it."
~ Theresa Ream

Don't make the mistake of trying to be connected to everyone. Real power doesn't come from popularity; it comes from alignment.

My client Marianne came to me exhausted, not because she wasn't doing enough, but because she was doing too much of the *wrong* thing.

On paper, she looked incredibly successful. She was a seasoned consultant with a solid reputation, years of experience, and a genuine desire to grow her business to the next level. Her calendar was full. Her weekdays were booked with mixers, luncheons, women's groups, chambers, associations, and networking events. She collected business cards like proof of effort. And yet, she felt invisible.

"I don't understand," she said in one of our early sessions. "I'm everywhere. I show up. I follow up. I post. I coffee-meet. But nothing meaningful comes from it. I'm tired, and honestly, I feel a little rejected."

What she didn't realize yet was that she was networking *outward* instead of aligning *inward*.

Marianne had been taught the traditional rule: more rooms, more people, more exposure. So, she blanketed her energy across anyone who might be useful someday. But feminine power doesn't work that way. Power, especially sustainable power, is built through resonance, not reach.

As we dug deeper, a pattern emerged: Marianne was contorting herself to fit into rooms that were never designed for her. She felt like she was an actress on stage. She led with credentials instead of conviction. She tried to be "interesting enough" to earn attention rather than simply being herself. Networking had become a performance instead of a connection.

I asked her a simple question: "Who actually *sees* you? Who really knows you?"

She paused. Her eyes filled with tears. "I don't think anyone really does."

That was the turning point.

We shifted her focus from *networking* to *allies*.

Instead of asking, "Who can I meet?" She began asking, "Who do I trust? Who energizes me? Who already believes in my work without needing to be convinced?" We identified just five women, not the loudest or most influential on paper, but the ones who felt like home. Women who asked real questions. Women who followed through. Women who spoke her name in rooms she wasn't in. Women with some of the same interests, goals, and values.

Her homework wasn't to attend another event; it was to deepen five relationships.

She scheduled intentional one-on-one conversations, not sales calls, not pitches, just honest connections. She shared her vision without polishing it. She spoke openly about where she was growing and where she felt unsure. And something unexpected happened: instead of losing credibility, she gained loyalty.

One of those women invited her to cohost a small workshop. Another introduced her to a client who turned into a long-term contract. Another simply became a sounding board, helping Marianne refine her voice and pricing with clarity and confidence.

Within six months, Marianne was working less and earning more. But the real shift wasn't financial; it was energetic. She stopped feeling like she had to chase opportunity. Opportunity started coming to her through trust.

"I finally understand," she said during a later session. "I wasn't meant to be everywhere. I was meant to connect."

What Marianne learned, and what so many women miss, is that blanket networking spreads your energy thin, while allies multiply it. Networking asks you to be impressive; allies ask you to be real. Networking trades in potential; allies trade in commonality and mutual respect.

She still attends events now, but differently. She no longer walks into rooms asking, "Who needs to see me?" She walks in anchored, asking, "Who feels aligned?" And if no one does, she leaves without making it mean anything about her worth.

Marianne didn't grow her business by collecting more contacts. She grew it by cultivating relationships, trust, and shared values. She stopped building a list and started building a circle.

That is feminine power at work. And that only happens when you stop networking for approval and start choosing allies from alignment.

You don't need a crowd; you need a few people who are all in.

- People who believe in you
- People who understand your mission
- People who want to see you win

You can only nurture a handful of true alliances at a time. Why? Because real allyship requires presence, attention, and reciprocity. These are not surface-level acquaintances or LinkedIn connections. True allies are the people you invest in and who invest in you, not out of obligation, but because there is a mutual recognition of value.

The deeper the connection, the greater the power exchange. A single trusted ally can open doors, steady you in crisis, and call you back to your truth when you're tempted to shrink. But that level of trust and intimacy doesn't happen when you're stretched across dozens of shallow relationships. It comes from choosing a few and going deep.

Think of it this way: A thousand flickering candles will give off light, but one roaring fire will warm you, sustain you, and draw others close. Allies are like that fire. When you commit to cultivating a few strong bonds, the power between you multiplies, and ideas flow more freely, resources are shared more generously, and opportunities show up more often.

In a world that constantly tells us to "network more" or "build bigger circles," the feminine path of power reminds us that influence is not measured in numbers but in depth. It's not about how many hands you shake; it's about how many souls you truly connect with.

That's why I love going on retreats with my business girlfriends. I recently attended a beautiful retreat in California hosted by my friend and mentor Tracie. She put us up in a big house at a quiet retreat facility in the redwoods of the Santa Cruz Mountains, a place where we walked among giant groves of trees, laughed and told stories around a fire, and sat by the pond writing out our plans. It was so quiet that it drowned out all the noise of business and family responsibilities. We sat around the kitchen table in our comfy clothes, coffee mugs in hand, laughing so hard our stomachs hurt one minute and we were wiping away tears the next. In that circle, titles and achievements didn't matter. What mattered was honesty, sharing the fears we carried, the risks we were about to take, and the dreams we weren't brave enough to say out loud anywhere else. By the time the retreat ended, each of us left with more than new strategies for our businesses; we carried home the certainty that we weren't walking this road alone. That's the power of true allies: They remind you of your strength when you've forgotten, and they hold your vision until you can believe in it again.

Why Relationships Matter More Than Requests

People help people they feel connected to. It's that simple. No one wants to be used. Nothing turns someone off faster than a cold request from someone who's never invested a moment in the relationship.

To build allies, you must build *relationships first.*

That means:

- Taking the time to listen
- Being genuinely interested in their world
- Giving support without needing anything back
- Sharing life, laughter, stories, and values

Allyship grows through *connection*, not convenience.

One of the most powerful ally relationships I've nurtured over the last four years has been with my speaking coach, Caterina. I attended her speaking retreat in the beautiful Napa Valley, Calif. It was the very first time I traveled without my husband, and I felt completely out of place. Public speaking terrified me. I was so nervous that I broke down in front of the group. It was embarrassing, but something magical happened. Instead of judgment, the other women rallied around me with encouragement and compassion. Caterina, in particular, saw beyond my fear and called out the voice and presence she knew I could grow into.

That moment was the start of an allyship that has shaped my life in ways I couldn't have imagined. Caterina not only coached me through my fear of speaking but also invited me into experiences that expanded my confidence, like women's cruises where I met extraordinary peers, practiced my voice, and built lasting friendships. Today, I speak frequently to women's groups with ease and joy. Well, the joy part is easy, but the ease I am still working on. And every time I take the microphone, I think back to that first retreat and the ally who saw my potential before I could see it myself. Our relationship continues to grow through new adventures, and I know she will always be one of my greatest allies.

The Anatomy of a Powerful Allyship

To build an allyship that endures and uplifts, four elements must be present: enjoying one another's company, mutual respect, shared experiences, and a mutual relationship.

1. Enjoying One Another's Company

It's not about being best friends, but there needs to be a real connection. Shared energy. Mutual enjoyment. If being around someone drains you, that person is not an ally. Allies nourish each other.

2. Mutual Respect

Respect is the cornerstone of power-sharing. Your allies should admire the way you move through the world. They believe in your work, your worth, and your words, and you believe in theirs.

Power doesn't flow where respect is absent.

3. Shared Experiences that Build Trust

Trust is built over time through experiences. Collaborating on projects. Supporting one another through change. Showing up consistently. Trust turns acquaintances into allies.

4. A Two-Way Relationship

Powerful allyship is *mutual*. Both parties give and receive, without keeping score. There's generosity, not obligation. You both know: *If I win, you win too.*

Who Are Your Allies?

In Work:
- Mentors who offer wisdom and guidance
- Managers who champion you for leadership roles
- Colleagues who publicly support your ideas and efforts
- Sponsors who promote you when you're not in the room

In Life:
- Friends who listen, encourage, and remind you of who you are
- Spouses or family who believe in your mission and vision
- Clients or followers who invest in and promote your brand
- Business partners who share your values and complement your strengths

That's the power of a true ally: They open doors that no amount of solo striving can.

Reflection: Candles or Fire?

Imagine your relationships as a source of light. Many connections are like candles, brief sparks that provide a little glow but fade quickly when the wind changes. True allies are like a fire: sustaining, warm, and powerful enough to draw people in and keep them close.

Journaling prompts to explore:

- Which of my current relationships feels more like candles than a fire, nice but fleeting?
- Which relationships burn like a fire, offering steady warmth, trust, and mutual growth?
- Where am I spreading myself too thin, tending too many small flames instead of nurturing a few strong fires?
- Who are the three to five people I want to invest in more deeply as allies this year?

Remember: depth creates durability. The more you feed the fire, the more it sustains you in return.

Action Steps: Building and Honoring Your Allies

- **Deepen a Key Relationship**
  Choose one current ally. Invite them for coffee. Send a thoughtful message. Ask how *you* can support *them*.
- **Identify a Missing Ally**
  What type of support are you missing? Strategic guidance? Emotional support? Brand amplification? Identify someone who could become that ally.
- **Initiate Authentically**
  Reach out with sincerity. Comment on their work. Offer something of value. Start the relationship from a place of curiosity and connection.
- **Reciprocate without Keeping Score**
  Offer support without needing recognition. Make it a habit to be generous in small ways.

Allies are part of your power infrastructure. They lift your vision, protect your time, and help you grow, not because they owe you, but because you've built something real with them.

Build slowly. Give deeply. Choose wisely. A few powerful relationships will always take you further than a thousand casual connections.

How to Attract the Right Allies

You don't chase powerful allies; you *magnetize* them. And the way to do that is by becoming someone whose energy, clarity, and integrity naturally draw others in. When you're deeply rooted in your mission, embodying your values, and showing up with presence and purpose, people notice. The right allies are not attracted to neediness or performance; they're drawn to alignment. They're watching how you lead, how you treat others, and how you speak about your vision. It's not about how perfect you are, but how *real* you are.

To attract powerful allies, you must **live your power out loud**. Share your story. Show your heart. Speak your truth with grace. When others see you walking in integrity, they want to walk with you. Be generous with your praise, consistent in your energy, and grounded in your value. There is no faster way to attract allies than by being one, without expectation, without keeping score. Givers recognize givers. Builders recognize builders. The more you embody the kind of ally you wish to attract, the more natural those relationships become.

And don't forget the power of visibility. People can't support what they can't see. Put yourself in rooms where aligned energy lives. Join communities, attend retreats, show up to conversations with intention. Be willing to be seen, not just for what you do, but for who you are. That's what creates a true connection. Allies aren't just looking for results; they're looking for committed connections. And when you shine from a place of wholeness, you won't have to go looking for allies; they'll be looking for you.

Discernment: One of the Most Underused Feminine Powers

You don't need to be paranoid, but you do need to be clear. Protecting your energy and your vision means being wise about who gets close. Trust is earned. Loyalty is proven. And your time is sacred.

Discernment is one of the most potent and under-celebrated feminine powers you possess. It's that quiet, intuitive knowing that happens beneath the surface, before logic kicks in. It's the ability to feel what's true, even when words and appearances try to convince you otherwise. Discernment isn't judgment; it's clarity. It's the power to say, *This energy is not for me,* without needing evidence or explanation. For centuries, women were taught to ignore this inner knowing, to play nice, to override their gut. But when you reclaim your intuitive authority, you stop letting performance fool you and start letting energy guide you.

To sharpen your discernment, practice listening *before* reacting. Watch what people do, not just what they say. Notice how your body responds around them: tight or open, expanded or small. Pay attention to patterns, not moments. The more you honor your instincts, the stronger they become. In a world full of curated personas and surface-level alliances, discernment becomes your divine compass, pointing you toward aligned partnerships, honest allies, and safe spaces to grow your power. You don't have to be loud to be wise; you just have to listen ... to *you*.

When it's Not Real: Spotting False Allies Early

Not everyone who smiles in your direction is on your side.

Not everyone who offers help has pure intentions.

And not everyone who seems supportive will remain that way when your light gets brighter.

Part of standing in your power is learning to recognize the difference between **true allies** and **performative ones**, those who *appear* to be on your side but are quietly competing, manipulating, or undermining you.

This doesn't mean walking around with suspicion; it means walking with **discernment**.

Look for Signs of Their True Motives

"A person's motives shape the relationship long before their words do. Often, we don't see how we've been influenced until it's already cost us something sacred: our time, our energy, or our truth."
~ Theresa Ream

Discernment means being willing to look beyond the surface and tune in to what someone's *real* motives might be. Many of us take people at face value because it feels easier or more comfortable in the moment, but feminine power invites us to look deeper. Not with suspicion, but with awareness. Sometimes people show up with praise, support, or opportunity, but underneath it is a need for control, validation, or access to your influence. We often miss the signs because we don't *want* to see them. But true discernment requires you to trust what your body is picking up, even when your mind is still trying to be polite. Pay attention to how someone behaves when you say no, when you shine, or when you stop needing them. Motives don't always speak; they reveal themselves in patterns. A person's motives shape the relationship and quietly influence what we do for them, often in ways we don't recognize until it's too late.

Signs Someone Is *Not* a True Ally

1. They only support you when you're not a threat.
If someone claps for you *until* you grow beyond them or get too visible, that's not an ally; that's a conditional supporter.

2. They never bring your name into rooms of opportunity.
Allies advocate. Performers stay silent. If they have access but never open the door for you, take note.

3. Their compliments feel like veiled comparisons.
"Wow, I never thought you'd do that!" or "That's so good, for someone like you." If it leaves you doubting yourself, it's not true support.

4. They only show up when they need something.
Real allies are consistent, not transactional. They check in without an agenda.

5. They gossip about others to you.
If they gossip *with* you, they'll likely gossip *about* you. True allies protect your name even when you're not listening.

6. They undermine your confidence subtly.
They might joke about your ambition, your ideas, or your goals, but it never lands right. These "jokes" are often jabs wrapped in humor.

I saw a friend learn, painfully and quietly, that not every ally is real. It didn't come from a romantic relationship; it came from someone she called an old friend, mentor, and supporter.

She had been open about her dreams, what she was building, how she was growing, the courage it took for her to step into a bigger life. And at first, the support was there. Encouragement. The affirming words. The sense of *we're in this together*.

But when her growth became visible, something shifted. When opportunities came her way, the room grew quiet; most would not have even noticed. When her name should have been spoken in rooms of possibility, it wasn't. Compliments began to land strangely, wrapped in surprise or comparison instead of shared pride. And slowly, subtly, she began to doubt herself.

What broke her heart wasn't a single moment of betrayal, but discovering that the closeness she felt was one-sided. While she celebrated her friend's wins, shared her ideas, and opened her world, the other woman was quietly keeping score. She wasn't cheering; she was collecting. Every vulnerable moment, every shared dream, every success became something to measure herself against. And when the moment came for true support, for sisterhood, for showing up, she didn't. She pulled back. Or worse, she positioned herself just close enough to benefit but never close enough to protect. That's what hurts. Not the loss of friendship, but the loss of what she thought it was. The realization that what felt like sisterhood had been a silent competition all along.

It was the slow realization that the person she thought was standing beside her was standing just behind her, watching, measuring, competing to make her move and use my friend's momentum for herself.

I remember the day she finally said, "I think she wanted me to stay small, but ride on my coattails to move herself forward." That sentence carried more grief than anger.

Letting go wasn't dramatic. It was devastating in a quieter way. She had to mourn not only the friendship but the illusion of safety she believed it held. She had to accept that shared history does not always mean shared intention.

And in that loss, she learned something profound: True allies don't flinch when your light grows brighter. They don't go silent when your success becomes real, while they quietly plot to edge ahead of you. They don't make you question your worth under the guise of friendship. They don't give you bad advice as pawns move.

False allies don't always push you down. Sometimes, they simply stop lifting you up and hope you won't notice while they move in a different direction, all the while looking for their next person to attach to. Watching her heal reminded me of this truth: Discernment is not distrust; it is self-protection to a very high degree.

How to Spot the Real Ones Earlier, Rather than Later

Use the lens of **behavior over time**. Words can be charming, but energy never lies. Look for:

- **Consistency**—They show up the same way whether you're winning or struggling.
- **Integrity**—They treat others well, not just you. I never continue a relationship with someone who is demeaning the wait staff!
- **Boundaries**—They respect yours and honor their own.

- **Joy in Your Wins**—They're genuinely *excited* for your elevation, not just tolerating it.
- **Reciprocity**—They give *and* receive without tracking a scoreboard

"Your power lies in your discernment; let your intuition speak louder than how others present themselves."
~ Theresa Ream

True allies don't need to convince you. You feel their alignment in your nervous system, in your body. It feels safe. Clean. Steady. You can breathe in their presence. That's your cue.

Build Trust to Strengthen Your Advocates and Cheerleaders

In the realm of feminine power, influence isn't seized; it's earned. And the currency that fuels this power isn't fear or force; its trust and showing up consistently.

Feminine allyship is relational, not positional. It's not about titles, achievements, or who talks the loudest in the room. It's about who people *feel safe* coming alongside of. Who they believe. Who they *want* to see win. You don't gain advocates and cheerleaders by asserting dominance. You gain them by embodying integrity, by becoming someone others can count on when it matters most.

People rally around consistency, not perfection. They trust the one who does what she says, shows up how she promises, and leads with both strength and soul. Trust is the invisible foundation that makes people want to carry your name, your brand, and your mission into rooms you haven't even entered yet. And when trust is strong, it turns colleagues into collaborators and friends into fierce advocates.

In business, life, and friendships, your circle is your power base. The woman who tries to rise alone will burn out. But the woman who nurtures genuine relationships, who builds others as she builds herself, will rise on the shoulders of a tribe that believes in her. Powerhouse women don't isolate themselves; they know how to be part of something bigger.

Getting to the top isn't about climbing over others; it's about creating enough momentum that others *want* to lift you. Because they've seen your integrity. Because you've celebrated their wins. Because you've shown up for them without keeping score.

Trust Turns Your Allies into Amplifiers

When people trust you as an ally, they become invested in your success. They promote your work. They speak your name in circles of opportunity. They watch your growth like it's their own, because in some ways, it is.

You build this kind of circle not through performance, but through presence. Be generous without attachment. Be honest without ego. Be consistent without needing recognition. These are the quiet qualities that make women unforgettable and deeply respected.

Feminine power doesn't dominate; it elevates. It doesn't hoard; it multiplies. When you show up in your truth, you create space for others to do the same. And that shared truth becomes a bond stronger than any business card, pitch, or promise.

The future is built on networks of trust. The more you lead with authenticity, the more people will want to walk beside you, which is always better than following you.

Even Wolves Hunt in Packs

A Client Story: Sherry Found Her Pack

Sherry had always been the strong one. The one who could figure it out, power through, keep the plates spinning. On the outside, she looked like she had it all together: successful career, well-managed home, and good instincts. But inside, she was lonely. Not isolated in the physical sense—she was surrounded by people—but *alone in vision*. No one really understood the kind of woman she was becoming. And the truth she didn't want to admit? She was exhausted from trying to hold it all together without being truly seen or heard by trusted confidants.

One day, after yet another business mastermind left her feeling like she had to shrink or compete, she whispered to herself: *There has to be a different way*. That whisper became a prayer. And that prayer became a path.

She stopped trying to network and started listening to her intuition. She began showing up more vulnerably in the right spaces, not the ones that looked impressive, but the ones that felt *safe*. She stopped trying to prove herself and started sharing her truth. Slowly, a few women noticed Women who weren't intimidated by her light. Women who didn't compete but contributed. Women who saw her, *all* of her, and chose to stand beside her anyway.

They weren't flashy. They weren't loud. But they were *real*. And over time, these women became her pack. They brainstormed ideas, held her accountable, reminded her who she was, and called her higher when she doubted herself. They didn't need her to dim. They needed her to *rise* because when she rose, *they did too*.

With her pack in place, Sherry finally launched the retreat she'd been dreaming of for five years. And it sold out in three weeks *without a funnel*. Why? Because her circle had already been amplifying her voice, her truth, and her energy for months. They weren't just allies. They were her *advocates*.

Now, she's not just successful in her offers; she's supported. She's not just visible; she's *held*. She doesn't walk alone anymore. Because she finally understood that even wolves hunt in packs.

So, build your pack. With care. With clarity. With women who don't just cheer for you but hold you up.

This is the feminine way. This is your power.

Action Plan: Building and Nurturing Your Allies

If your power is the house, your allies are the foundation, scaffolding, and lighting. They expand what you're capable of and reflect your brilliance to you when you forget. But strong allies don't just *happen*; they're cultivated through discernment, energy, and aligned action.

Here's how to build your circle with power, purpose, and intention.

1. Audit Your Current Circle

Start by identifying who is currently around you. Who energizes you? Who drains you? Who do you trust to hold your vision with care, and who has made it about themselves but masqueraded as a supporter?
Ask yourself:

- Who consistently supports me, without condition or agenda?
- Who has shown up for me during a challenge or transition?
- Who promotes my growth, my ideas, or my business?

After answering the above questions, is it time to expand or change the types of people you want in your ally circle?

Now that you've taken inventory, begin to define the kind of energy and presence you want more of. You're not just looking for people who like you; you're calling in those who challenge you with love, celebrate your brilliance without jealousy, and hold space for your vision without shrinking your voice. Look for people who embody values you admire: integrity, consistency, generosity, and joy. You want mentors who have walked the path, collaborators who match your fire, and friends who remind you of your truth when you forget. Your circle should include people who expand your thinking, protect your peace, and help you rise to your next level, not just keep you comfortable in your current one. These are your *true* allies, and their presence will shape your future.

These are your existing allies. You may have fewer than you thought, or more. The clarity will guide you forward.

2. Identify the Gaps

Now ask: What kind of support am I missing?
You may need:

- A **mentor** to stretch your strategy
- A **collaborator** to help bring your vision to life
- A **connector** who can introduce you to new rooms
- An **emotional supporter** who sees the *real* you

When you know what's missing, you can attract and align with the people who carry what you need and have a mutual desire for growth and impact.

3. Build Before You Ask

Never build relationships just to "use" them. Instead, be intentional. Show up first with presence not pitch.
Ways to build trust:

- Send a sincere compliment or message of appreciation
- Promote their work if it aligns with your values
- Invite them to collaborate or share ideas, with no pressure
- Offer value before asking for support

Energy doesn't lie. People can feel when you're building connections with integrity.

4. Deepen Your Anchor Allies

Choose three key people to intentionally deepen your relationship with. These may be current mentors, friends, or collaborators you admire. Schedule time to check in. Ask how you can support *them*. Share your vision and ask for wisdom, not favors.

Long-term allies are built over time, not in convenience.

5. Be the Ally You Want to Attract

Everything in feminine leadership is reciprocal. If you want support, show up in support. If you want trust, be trustworthy. If you want loyalty, demonstrate consistency.

Ask yourself:

- Where can I celebrate another woman this week?
- Who needs encouragement or spotlight?
- What energy am I bringing to my relationship?

When you embody what you seek, the right allies will naturally align with you.

Your Assignment

- Name five current allies
- Reach out to one person you'd like to deepen your relationship with
- Identify one type of ally you're calling in (mentor, friend, partner, etc.)
- Do one generous act, no agenda, just aligned giving

This is how feminine power grows: not in isolation, but in intention.

Build your circle. Anchor in trust. Let them help lift you as you rise higher than you ever could alone.

Chapter Four: The Law of Alchemizing Your Gifts

"What if living your purpose was more important than the opinions of others?"
~ Theresa Ream

Every woman carries a brilliance that is uniquely her own: a quiet genius, often disguised as a quirk, a curiosity, or a way of seeing the world that no one else does. Yet somewhere between our natural spark and the pressures of achievement, many of us lose sight of that brilliance. We begin to trade our originality for acceptance. We follow "proven systems," copy successful formulas, and polish ourselves into versions that look right, sound right, and feel utterly wrong.

But power doesn't live in perfection; it lives **alchemizing** or transforming the raw material of who you are into something luminous, valuable, and alive.

This law reminds us that our true magic lies not in becoming more like others but in daring to become more deeply ourselves.

The Cost of Conformity

"Your success accelerates when your business reflects who you are, not who you were told to be."
~ Theresa Ream

There was a time when I believed the secret to success was imitation. I modeled my business after others who seemed to have it all figured out, mimicking their language, leadership style, and marketing structures. I thought if I could just master their formula, I'd find the same success.

When I stepped into an industry where I clearly did not fit the mold, I quickly realized the restoration world was male-dominated and fueled by bravado. When I began marketing my business to insurance agents, I could have tried to match that energy, but instead I chose to lead with relationship, integrity, and quiet confidence, and it felt completely aligned with who I was. So instead of conforming, I trusted my instincts and chose a different path. I began showing up with warmth instead of words. I brought thoughtful, themed treats during the holidays. I added simple, cheerful décor to brighten their offices. I didn't talk about my business until they asked. I simply attached a business card and let the experience speak for itself. Something unexpected happened: The agents, adjusters, and brokers remembered me. They looked forward to my visit. When I missed a stop, a few called the office asking where I was. Eventually, they began asking questions, and then they began sending work. That one intuitive shift, born from refusing to conform, built millions in revenue and continues to do so more than forty-five years later. Today, I have a marketing team of women and men who carry that same non-conforming, relationship-first approach into the field. This is what happens when you honor your nature instead of copying someone else's; you don't just stand out, you become unforgettable.

Conformity is seductive because it promises safety. When you suppress what's original within you, you dim the very light that draws opportunity, prosperity, and joy toward you.

I stopped trying to be like others in my industry and started working from my gift of nurturing. I looked inward. I began to ask myself: *What lights me up? What feels natural? What drains me completely?*

*"What felt natural to me became unforgettable to them.
That difference built my legacy, and it can build yours
too."*
~ Theresa Ream

That season taught me that success does not come from imitating others, long before I had language for it. It came from living in my strengths. While others tried to impress with words, credentials, and bravado, I quietly subtracted what did not feel natural to me. I did not explain. I did not pitch. I did not perform. I allowed presence to replace persuasion and warmth to replace ego. In doing so, I discovered something profound: When you stop trying to be seen the way others are seen, you become remembered for who you truly are.

That was the moment **I discovered the power of subtraction: the sacred act of clearing away everything that was never truly me**. Not by adding more strategies or trying harder, but by gently releasing what felt forced, performative, or borrowed. With each layer I removed, I came closer to myself. In that quiet, my own genius became clear. I finally understood what it means to live and work from your genius zone.

This is what happens when you stop becoming someone else and return to who you have always been. Subtraction does not diminish your power; it reveals it.

As the noise fell away, clarity returned. Opportunities no longer felt chased; they appeared. The right people found me: collaborators, team members, and clients who resonated with my company's values and our way of being. Ideas arrived with ease, and the energy around work shifted from tension to trust.

I stopped living in a constant state of worry and second-guessing. Instead, I learned to listen to what is important. Processes that once felt complicated began to organize themselves. The business found its natural flow. What had once felt heavy became elegant. What once required force now responded to presence.

And then one morning, without fanfare or fireworks, I realized something simple and powerful: I was happy. Not chasing happiness. Not striving for contentment. Simply living it. I felt grounded, whole, and at ease with my choices. This is the quiet reward of alignment, not just success, but peace. Not just growth, but joy.

The Power of Intriguing Identity

You are not here to compete; you are here to stand apart.

So many women are taught to scan the room, assess the market, and adjust themselves accordingly. To ask, *Who do I need to be to be chosen? What do I need to say to be taken seriously? How do I need to show up to belong?* But feminine power does not come from adaptation. It comes from **distinction through embodiment or intriguing identity**.

Your uniqueness is not found in your product, your service, or even your credentials. It lives in something far less replicable. It lives in your energy. In the way you approach life. In the values you refuse to compromise. In the tone of your leadership. In the story your presence tells before you ever speak a word.

"Long before anyone understands what you do, they feel who you are."
~ Theresa Ream

For me, that intriguing identity reveals itself in my company's culture. My husband and I believe in building people to be the best they can be through support. It's not just about leading teams; our culture sculpts champions. I see potential where others see roles, and I treat leadership like an art form, not a hierarchy. Leaders are built the way a promoter grooms a fighter, not by tearing them down, but by sharpening their confidence, strengthening their presence, and training them to trust themselves.

Watching people rise is not just something I enjoy; it is part of my nature. It is how my power expresses itself. I thrive on developing leaders who can stand on their own, speak with clarity, and carry themselves with quiet authority. I don't need followers who depend on me. I want leaders who expand beyond me.

That same identity shows up in our company's marketing, how we serve, and how we build businesses. I love building out a marketing team that touches hearts, not just sells or promotes. We design customer experiences that make people feel remembered, not sold to. We approach finances with both discipline and intuition, blending metrics with creativity. Strategy matters, but soul always leads.

And I am fiercely protective of my genius zone. Anything that pulls me into depletion, distraction, or is forced in any way gets delegated or omitted. I have learned that genius is sustainable, and exhaustion is not. Feminine power does not come from doing everything. It comes from doing what you were uniquely designed to do and letting the rest fall into capable hands.

This is not arrogance or passing the buck; it's alignment with your natural gifts.

Alignment is knowing where your power lives and refusing to abandon it for approval. It is choosing to lead from your natural rhythm instead of forcing yourself into models that were never built for you. It is understanding that when you honor your identity, your business becomes lighter, clearer, and more profitable.

When you live and lead from your unique energetic blueprint, something subtle but powerful happens: You become magnetic. Clients do not need convincing because they can feel your authenticity. Partners respect your clarity because you are not posturing or proving. Your team trusts your leadership because it is grounded and consistent. Your business begins to mirror your vitality instead of draining it.

This is the kind of identity that cannot be copied.

No one else can replicate the way you think, the way you connect, the way you hold space, or the way you make people feel. And when you stop trying to compete on surface-level attributes and start leading from essence, comparison loses its grip. You stop asking, *How do I measure up?* And start asking, *How do I express what is already true?*

This is the essence of alchemy.

No woman embodies the power of intriguing identity more clearly than Coco Chanel. She did not simply design clothing; she redesigned what it meant to be a woman in the world. At a time when fashion was restrictive, ornamental, and built for the male gaze, Chanel infused her own values into her work: freedom, simplicity, confidence, and self-possession. Her designs mirrored how she lived. Unconstrained. Independent. Mirroring herself. Chanel didn't ask what women wanted to wear. She created what *she* needed to feel powerful, and in doing so, she liberated generations of women. Her brand became iconic not because it followed trends, but because it carried her essence: the mark of true feminine power. When a woman allows her identity to shape her creation, the result is not just a business, but a legacy.

Alchemizing your identity means turning the truth of who you are into value, impact, and prosperity. It means allowing your natural gifts, your lived experiences, your perspective, and your presence to become the foundation of your leadership and your work. Not by polishing yourself into something marketable, but by revealing yourself more fully.

The most intriguing women do not try to be impressive. They are deeply rooted. They know who they are. They trust their way of seeing the world. And because of that, others are drawn to them, not by force, but by resonance.

Your identity is not something you need to invent. It is something you need to remember. And when you do, power stops being something you chase and becomes something you embody.

That alchemy is the power of intriguing identity.

Alignment Moment:

Irreplaceability is not achieved through perfection or conformity, but through the courage to embody your own way of being. Where in your life or business have you been blending in when you were meant to stand apart?

Build a Business That Mirrors Your Life Vision

"When your work reflects who you are, your legacy writes itself."
~ Theresa Ream

Most women don't start businesses to build empires; they start them to build freedom. Freedom to spend time with family, to travel, to create impact, to birth an idea, to make their own decisions and to live a life that feels abundant and alive.

But somewhere along the way, the business starts running them. The dream gets buried beneath the to-do list. The very thing meant to bring freedom begins to feel like a cage.

The shift comes when you realize you're not just building a business; you're designing a life.

When I reimagined my companies, I began by imagining my ideal life. I saw myself traveling with family, owning fast muscle cars, soaking up sunshine in a second home in a warm climate, coaching and leading women entrepreneurs, and being a top-notch CEO for The Ream Companies. I wanted my work to fuel that vision, not fight against it.

So, I rebuilt my business to support my rhythm and my vision. I delegated operations to a trusted team, automated what drained me, and kept my focus on people, strategy, and vision, my natural genius zones. The moment I aligned my business with my desired lifestyle, everything began to flow with ease.

That's the feminine way of building: **life first, business second.**

A Client Story: When You Choose Yourself

One of my private clients came to me after building a highly successful service-based business. From the outside, it looked impressive: strong revenue, a full calendar, a respected reputation. But in our first conversation, she quietly admitted, "I built exactly what everyone told me to build ... and I don't recognize my life anymore. I feel like I have totally lost control of my life."

Her days were packed with meetings she dreaded, operational details she hated, and constant availability that left no room for creativity, rest, or joy. The business that was supposed to create freedom had slowly become a binding weight.

Instead of asking how to scale or optimize, I asked her a different question: "What do you want your life to feel like?"

She described slow mornings, time to travel, afternoons free for movement and reflection, and work that felt meaningful instead of draining. She envisioned having control of her time back. None of those desires were reflected in her current business model. So, we began again, not by adding more, but by subtracting.

Together, we eliminated offers that no longer aligned, delegated responsibilities that pulled her out of her genius, and redesigned her schedule around her natural rhythm. She shifted into higher-value work that allowed her to serve deeply without overextending. Within months, she was working fewer hours, earning more, and, most importantly, waking up with a sense of peace instead of pressure.

The business didn't shrink when she chose herself; it expanded. Because when a woman designs her business around her life, instead of sacrificing her life for her business, everything comes back into harmony.

This is the feminine way of building: intuitive, intentional, and aligned with who you truly are.

The Blueprint of Alignment

Living this law is about creating a structure that supports your soul, not one that suffocates it. These guiding principles will help you alchemize your gifts into profit, without losing your peace.

Design for Lifestyle

You are not building a business to escape your job; you are designing the architecture of your freedom. Create offers, schedules, and systems that honor the way you want to live. Build in rest. Build in joy. Build space to breathe.

Focus on Your Genius

Anything that consistently drains you is not your genius. Delegate it, automate it, or delete it. The world doesn't need you exhausted; it needs you to be alive. Your genius is the zone where your talent, joy, and impact intersect with a customer's needs. Stay there.

Build Systems That Serve You

Feminine power thrives in flow, but flow needs a container. Systems are the masculine structure that allows your creative energy to move freely without chaos. Streamline. Simplify. Automate. Train your people well. Then trust them. Systems run the business; people run the systems.

Set Nonnegotiable

Boundaries are not barriers; they are declarations of worth. Protect your time, your energy, and your joy fiercely. For me, that means no meetings during workout times, sacred vacations with family, and owning at least eighty percent of my calendar. When you honor your non-negotiables, the world learns to honor you.

Align Offers with Purpose and Profit

"Every offer carries your energy. When it's aligned, people feel it before they understand it."
~ Theresa Ream

Never sell something that doesn't feel aligned, no matter how profitable it looks. Every offer you make is an energetic contract. If it doesn't feed your purpose *and* sustain your wealth, it will eventually drain both.

These principles are not rules; they are reminders that your business should be an expression of your soul, not a substitute for it.

My client, Nancy, came to me feeling quietly defeated. On the surface, her business looked active. Her free workshops were full. Women showed up, took notes, thanked her, and told her how inspiring she was. But when it came time to invite them into her paid offers, there was silence. No enrollment. No momentum. Just a growing ache in her chest that whispered, *What am I doing wrong?*

Over time, that silence began to erode her self-worth. She started questioning her value, her pricing, and even her gifts. She wondered if she needed to water herself down, add more bonuses, or create something "easier to say yes to." The truth was not that she lacked brilliance. It was that her offers were not aligned with her power. Her free workshops were alive because they were pure expression. Her paid offers reflected a false sense of obligation rather than the work she was meant to embody.

When we slowed everything down, I asked her a different question: "Does this offer feel like an expansion of you or a compromise of you?" She knew the answer. The offer she was trying to sell felt heavy. It was profitable on paper but disconnected from her purpose. She had unknowingly turned her business into a substitute for worth instead of an expression of soul.

Together, we released the misaligned offer. We rebuilt from her truth. We designed a paid experience that felt as nourishing as her free work, one that honored her depth, her boundaries, and her desire to serve without self-betrayal. The shift was immediate. Her energy changed, her invitations became clear and confident, and she naturally attracted the clients who were meant for her.

The next time she opened enrollment, women said yes. Not because she convinced them, but because they could feel her alignment. She wasn't selling anymore. She was inviting. And in that invitation, both her income and her confidence returned. People can feel when you are not aligned with what you are selling, and energetically, you can even make sure they don't buy it: Your energy will repel instead of attracting.

That is the power of aligning offers with purpose and profit. When what you sell feeds your soul and sustains your wealth, you stop chasing validation and start embodying value. Your business becomes a mirror of your truth, and the right people recognize it instantly.

Defining Your Identity

"Your identity becomes your compass. Define it. Name it.
Live by it."
~ Theresa Ream

You cannot monetize what you have not claimed.

Every brand, every leader, every woman who changes the world begins with identity. When you know who you are and what you stand for, every decision becomes clear.

Here is my business and life mission statement:

Mission: Grow the individual. Build the family. Inspire the community. Enrich the world.

How We Behave: We are fun, loyal, and passionate.

Success Principle: We deliver high-quality work on profitable jobs—always.

These aren't slogans that you see on corporate walls; they aren't just another saying that sounds good but that the business doesn't embody. They're the heartbeat of everything I do. When I'm faced with uncertainty or the temptation to chase trends, I return to them. They remind me who I am, and who I'm not.

Alignment in Practice: Defining Your Identity

Identity is not something you invent. It is something you remember and claim. Use the reflections below to anchor who you are, how you lead, and what you are here to build.

1. Claiming Your Core

When you strip away roles, titles, and expectations, who are you at your core?

What qualities do people consistently experience when they are around you?

Write without editing. Let truth lead; do not polish it.

2. Your Inner Compass

Think about a recent decision that felt heavy or confusing.

Which value of yours was being challenged or ignored in that moment?

What would have felt different if you had made that decision from alignment instead of approval?

3. From Words to Embodiment
Look at your current mission, values, or guiding principles.
Where are you fully living them?
Where are they aspirational but not yet embodied?
Identity becomes powerful when it is practiced, not just stated.

4. Behavior as Identity
How you behave when no one is watching reveals who you truly are.
In moments of stress, do your actions reflect your stated values or contradict them?
What would shift if you treated your behavior as your brand?

5. Success, Redefined
How do you personally define success beyond money or recognition?
What does success feel like in your body when you are living in alignment?
Is your current version of success nourishing you or draining you?

6. What You Are No Longer Available For
Identity is clarified as much by what you refuse as by what you choose.
What behaviors, clients, expectations, or compromises are you no longer willing to entertain?
Write a short list of non-negotiables that protect who you are becoming.

7. Naming Your Compass
Complete this statement in your own words:
"When I am unsure of my next step, I return to _______________ because it reminds me of who I am."
This is your compass. Let it guide you.

The Alchemy of Authenticity

When you stop trying to prove your worth and start embodying it, everything you touch begins to transform. There is a quiet shift that happens inside you. You no longer reach outward for validation or permission. Instead, you stand rooted in who you are. From that place, your presence alone begins to speak. You become the kind of leader who attracts opportunities rather than chases them. The kind of woman whose energy opens doors that hustle never could.

This is the essence of authenticity. It is not about trying harder or becoming more impressive. It is about allowing yourself to be fully seen as you are. When you stop performing for approval, your nervous system settles. Your decisions become easier. Your voice becomes steadier. And the world responds differently to you because you are no longer asking to be chosen. You are choosing yourself.

Alchemizing your gifts into profit is not about force; it is about frequency. It is about the energetic alignment that occurs when you are doing the work you were truly made to do. When your actions match your inner truth, your energy carries coherence. People feel it before they understand it. They trust it. They lean toward it. This is not strategy alone; this is resonance.

When you operate from that aligned energy, things begin to move with less resistance. Clients find you without being chased. Allies appear without being hunted. Ideas flow without being forced. Conversations open naturally. Opportunities arrive that you could not have planned or predicted. It can feel almost mystical, but it is deeply practical. You are no longer leaking energy trying to be someone else. All your power is finally moving in one direction.

This is what it means when we say the universe meets a woman who knows her power. It is not that life becomes perfect; it is that life becomes responsive. You notice how support shows up when you are no longer pushing against yourself. You trust your own timing. You trust your instincts. You trust your own authority. And because of that trust, you stop settling for what drains you and start saying yes to what sustains you.

The truth is—your gifts were never meant to sit quietly in the corner. They were never meant to be hidden, diluted, or rationed out of fear. Your gifts are meant to shine. They are meant to circulate through your work, your leadership, your creativity, and your relationships. They are meant to serve others, not at the expense of you, but in partnership with your well-being.

Money, in this context, is not the goal; it is the response. It becomes one of the many ways the world says thank you for what you are offering. When your gifts are shared from alignment rather than obligation, prosperity becomes a natural extension of service. You are no longer trading your energy for approval. You are allowing value to flow in both directions.

This is the alchemy of authenticity. When you live from your truth, power stops being something you chase and becomes something you embody. And from that place, everything you create carries meaning, impact, and lasting value.

Alignment in Practice

"What feels effortless is often where your greatest value lives."
~ Theresa Ream

Conforming will never make you exciting. It will not make you wealthy. And it will certainly not make you unforgettable. Conformity may feel safe, but it slowly disconnects you from the very essence that makes your work meaningful. When you shape yourself to fit expectations, you trade resonance for approval and ease for exhaustion.

Alignment lives in your zone of genius, that sacred intersection where joy, mastery, and ease meet. It is the place where work stops feeling like effort and starts feeling like expression. When you are operating from this space, you do not have to push or prove. Your energy is coherent. Your decisions are clearer. Flow begins naturally, and abundance expands without force.

Many women believe that success requires constant striving, endless output, and relentless hustle. But feminine power does not thrive in pressure; it thrives in rhythm. When you honor your natural pace and strengths, your work becomes sustainable and satisfying. You stop chasing outcomes and start allowing results to meet you where you are.

Alignment in practice begins with honest self-inquiry. Notice where your energy lifts and where it drains. Pay attention to the tasks that feel alive in your body versus the ones that feel heavy or forced. Effortless does not mean easy; it means true. It means your talents and timing are working together instead of against each other.

Ask yourself where you may be forcing outcomes instead of allowing them. Where are you pushing because you believe you should, rather than because it feels aligned? Where are you still conforming out of fear of being seen as too different, too fast, too slow, or too unconventional? These questions are not meant to judge you. They are meant to guide you home to yourself.

Imagine what your business would look like if it were built entirely around your natural rhythm and genius. Imagine choosing projects that energize you, structuring your days to support your well-being, and offering work that reflects who you truly are. This is not a fantasy; it is a practice, one small decision at a time.

You do not need to hustle harder to be powerful. You need to trust yourself more deeply. Feminine power grows when you move in alignment with your truth, honor your inner knowing, and allow flow to replace force. When you live and work this way, success stops feeling heavy and starts feeling inevitable.

Alignment is not something you reach someday; it is something you practice daily.

Reflection and Practice Guide

"Your gifts create impact when you allow them to be seen, valued, and exchanged." ~ Theresa Ream

Alchemizing Your Gifts into Power and Profit

Your gifts were never meant to sit quietly within you. They are meant to circulate through your work, your relationships, your art, and your leadership.

These exercises will help you uncover the essence of what makes you unique, release conformity, and design a business (and life) that mirrors your highest alignment.

1. The Excavation: Unearthing Your Genius

Take a deep breath and recall moments when you've felt most *alive* in your work, those times when you lose track of time, when creativity feels like oxygen.

Write down:

- What was I doing?
- Who was I serving or connecting with?
- What about that experience felt effortless and energizing?

Now notice the pattern. Those experiences point directly to your zone of genius, the place where your natural abilities and your purpose intersect.

Reflection Moment: How much of your current work is spent in that zone, and what would need to shift for you to spend more time there?

2. The Purge: Releasing What Drains You

Power leaks wherever your energy is misused. Every time you say yes to something that depletes you, you say no to your brilliance.

List the tasks, commitments, or relationships that consistently drain your energy. Circle the top three.

Ask yourself (for each of the three):

- Can I delegate this?
- Can I automate this?
- Can I lovingly release this?

Make one small commitment today to remove or reduce at least one energy drain from your schedule this week.

Reflection:

How does it feel in your body when you imagine letting it go? That sensation is your compass. Follow it.

3. The Mirror: Naming What Makes You Different

Every woman of power has an energetic fingerprint. Your uniqueness might be the way you lead, teach, create, heal, or inspire.

Answer these prompts:

- What do people naturally come to me for?
- What do I do differently, even if I've never thought much about it?
- When others describe me, what words do they use repeatedly?
- Where am I already magnetic without trying?

Alignment Moment: Your power often hides in what you take for granted. Claim it out loud:

"I am uniquely gifted in _________________, and I am ready to build from that."

4.   The Blueprint: Designing for Alignment

Close your eyes and visualize your ideal life: your mornings, your energy, your environment, your freedom. Now, imagine your business seamlessly woven into that vision.

Write down:

- What does my ideal day look like?
- How does my business support that day, not interrupt it?
- What boundaries protect my energy and joy?

Reflection: If something in your business feels heavy or forced, it's not in alignment. Ask yourself: *What small shift could I make this month to bring more ease, joy, or flow into my work?*

5.   The Claim: Declaring Your Identity

Your mission is your declaration to the world. It is your compass when doubt or noise threatens to pull you off course.

Using your own words, complete these statements:

- **My mission:** ________________________________
- **My core values:** ____________________________
- **The kind of impact I'm here to make:** ____________________________________
- **How I want people to feel when they work with me:** ________________________________

Reflection: When you know who you are and what you stand for, your offers, your clients, and your opportunities begin to align naturally.

6. The Embodiment: Taking Aligned Action

Knowledge without movement becomes stagnation. The feminine path is about embodied creation, acting from inner knowing, not pressure.

Choose one small but significant action that aligns with your gifts. It might be launching an offer that feels authentic, saying no to a misaligned client, delegating a draining task, or carving out time to create freely.

Reflection: Journal what happens when you move from alignment instead of obligation. How does life respond when you honor your genius?

7. The Alchemist's Affirmation

Stand, breathe deeply, and read this aloud:

I no longer hide my brilliance to make others comfortable.

I am the alchemist of my own gifts. My creativity, intuition, and courage are my currency.

Everything I create flows from my authentic power.

I was born to turn my gifts into gold, and I do so with grace, ease, and purpose.

Alignment Isn't a Luxury

Alignment is not the icing; it's the cake. It's the foundation of everything that feels free, prosperous, and meaningful.

You were never meant to mimic someone else's path. You were born to **alchemize your gifts into gold**, to turn the raw material of your life, your story, and your genius into something that serves the world and sustains your soul.

When you live by this law, profit becomes sacred. Business becomes an extension of purpose. And power becomes effortless.

You don't need to become more like them.

You need to become more like you.

You are not meant to fit in.

You are meant to *transform*.

You are meant for your brilliance to shine.

Each time you honor your truth, your alignment, and your calling, you turn ordinary work into art and ordinary effort into impact.

Remember, alchemizing your gifts is not a one-time event. It's a rhythm, a dance between who you are becoming and what you are creating. The more you trust that dance, the more life will rise to meet you in your power.

Chapter Five: The Law of Protecting Your Power

"Every boundary you set is an act of self-devotion: I choose me, I choose peace, I choose power."
~ Theresa Ream

Power doesn't always leave us in big, dramatic scenes. More often, it seeps away through subtle leaks; moments where someone's tone, silence, or sideways comment unsettles your confidence. These are the quiet hits of an emotional sniper. They don't shout. They don't argue. They aim for your energy with observation, precision, and stealth.

And here's the tricky part: Sometimes it isn't even intentional. A parent's warning, a friend's caution, or a partner's silence can carry unspoken fear. People often pass their insecurities on to us without realizing it. Whether deliberate or unconscious, the impact is the same: doubt, hesitation, or shrinking back. Protecting your power means learning to recognize these leaks, refusing to internalize them, and setting boundaries that keep your energy sovereign.

We expect to lose our footing out in the world, among critics, competitors, or strangers who don't see our brilliance.

What we rarely expect is to lose our power in the place meant to feel safe: in our homes, from the words or actions of a trusted mentor or loving parent.

And yet, it happens all the time.

The undermining here is subtle. Most of the time, it doesn't come with shouts or accusations. It arrives in whispers, silences, and sideways glances.

It doesn't hold you back by force; it watches you pause yourself to keep the peace.

These are the emotional snipers of our lives: the people we love, trust, or value, who sometimes, consciously or unconsciously, drain our energy, seed our doubt, or anchor us to old versions of ourselves.

A dear client of mine experiences this with her mother. Every time she shares a new accomplishment, a promotion, a trip she planned, even something simple like starting a wellness routine, her mom responds with a subtle dig: "Are you sure that's a good idea?" or "Don't get ahead of yourself." Instead of celebrating, her mom ties her to the image of the hesitant girl she once was, as if she hasn't grown at all.

One day, instead of shrinking or brushing it off, my client paused. She smiled gently and said, "I know you mean well, but I trust my choices now. I'd love your support in celebrating this with me."

The room went quiet. For the first time, her mom didn't have a comeback. And my client felt the shift, not because her mother suddenly changed, but because *she did.* She had drawn a sacred line. She refused to be anchored in the past, and in that moment, she stood fully as the woman she had become.

This is the essence of feminine power: not silencing others but no longer silencing yourself.

And the only shields we truly have against them are **sacred boundaries.**

Boundaries are not punishments or walls. They are rivers. They direct where love, energy, and respect can flow, and where they cannot. They protect the sanctity of your life.

The Homefront Snipers

"Some people don't need to raise their voice to lower your power. Protect your energy from the quiet snipers." ~
Theresa Ream

The Parent, Relative, or Old Friend Who Still "Knows Better"

In the outside world, disrespect can be brushed off. But at home, love is interwoven with identity. You expect sanctuary, not sabotage. That's why these arrows of doubt cut so deeply; they come from the hands you expect to hold you.

And yet, here is the truth: They can only wound you if you hand them the ammunition.

When you shrink, when you silence yourself, when you trade your joy for their comfort, you load the weapon for them.

"The moment you shrink to make someone feel comfortable; you've handed them the power that belongs to you." ~ Theresa Ream

Why It Hurts More at Home

The most painful snipers are rarely strangers. They are the people whose love matters most, the ones whose approval still touches tender places in our hearts. When a parent, partner, sibling, or lifelong friend questions us, doubts us, or subtly corrects us, it can cut deeper than open criticism. Their words carry history, memory, and emotional weight. A casual comment meant as concern can reopen old wounds and pull us back into former versions of ourselves that we have long outgrown. This kind of sniping hurts because it blurs love with limitation. We feel torn between honoring the relationship and honoring ourselves. Feminine power does not deny that pain. It recognizes it, tends to it, and chooses sovereignty anyway. Instead of shrinking to preserve harmony, we learn to stay rooted in who we are now, allowing love to exist without letting it define or diminish our power.

They may say things with authority, as if they know better than the woman you've become. They anchor you to the past, even though you've risen into your present strength.

The feminine response isn't to prove or argue. It is to stand calmly in your sovereignty. You can thank them for their care and gracefully change the subject, or simply say, *I'll take that into consideration.* And when the moment calls for greater clarity, you may need to be bold and declare: *Thank you. I do value your input and will take your advice into consideration.* See, no argument or taking a stance. That is power!

When you speak it aloud, you're not just addressing them; you're declaring sovereignty to yourself. You're not rejecting their love; you're inviting them to see you as the woman you've become.

Reflection Where in my life am I still allowing someone to speak to the old version of me, and how can I remind them, through my words, presence, or boundaries, of the woman I am today?

The Partner Who Withdraws Until You Give In

Silence becomes a weapon in relationships. It becomes a way to punish you without words, creating distance that leaves you scrambling to restore closeness. They retreat emotionally, leaving you to bend first, soften your stance, or abandon your truth for the illusion of harmony.

Silence in a relationship can feel like quicksand. Withdrawal pulls you into the pattern of over-giving, apologizing, or abandoning your truth just to restore closeness.

The feminine response is neither chasing nor collapsing. It is naming. You stand in presence and say: *I sense distance right now. I value our intimacy; I'll be here when you're ready.*

This shifts the dynamic. You stop participating in the silent standoff and instead invite a higher form of connection.

Boundaries here are not walls; they are invitations to authentic intimacy.

One of my clients, a brilliant entrepreneur, used to dread her husband's silences. Whenever tension arose, he would retreat into wordless withdrawal, sometimes for days. She found herself tiptoeing around the house, softening her opinions, even abandoning decisions in her business just to bring him back into conversation.

The silence worked; it bent her to his will.

One day, she tried something new. When the silence came, she didn't chase. Instead, she said gently: "I'm here for an honest conversation whenever you're willing. I believe we can work through this."

Then she picked up her journal and wrote, refusing to sit in the discomfort of waiting.

At first, he didn't respond. But when he realized she was no longer willing to carry the weight of his withdrawal, he returned ready to talk. She learned that her power was never in pulling him out of silence; it was in refusing to abandon herself to it.

The Adult Child Who Guilt-Trips or Disrespects You

Adult children know how to press the deepest buttons, and guilt is often their sharpest tool. Even when guilt has nothing to stand on, they will manipulate by turning to guilt tactics. They may frame your stances, ideas, or the way you choose to spend your time and resources as selfishness. They may demand "fairness" as leverage, pushing you to bend your boundaries or choices to suit their needs. And of course, your mother-heart aches, wanting to soothe.

But here's the truth: Choosing what is right for you isn't betrayal; it's protecting your power. And a powerful parent is a great role model.

You can say: *My choices do not diminish my love for you, and I know you want what's best for me and brings me happiness.*

This reframes the moment. You're doing your adult child a profound favor by modeling the strength that comes with personal power. You're showing them what it looks like to honor oneself without abandoning others.

One woman I coached had a grown son who constantly leaned on her financially. She was single and didn't have a lot of money to spare, but for some reason, he felt he was entitled to her money. He would do everything in his power to guilt her into handing it over. "If you really cared about me, you'd help," he'd say, leaving her torn between her role as a mother and her right to thrive as a woman.

Finally, she drew a line. When the next request came, she took a deep breath and said: "I love you, and I believe in your ability to figure this out."

It wasn't easy. He was frustrated at first. But over time, something shifted. He started taking more responsibility, and she felt lighter, more empowered. Her boundary not only protected her, but it also gave him space to grow. Sometimes our love for our children keeps them small, and it takes courage to step back and let them deal with natural consequences.

Handling Disrespect

All too often, adult children can show disrespect, like rolling their eyes, dismissing your words, making you feel old and out of touch or speaking in tones that strip you of dignity. The temptation is to either lash out or shrink back in silence. But feminine power does neither. Instead, you hold steady. You meet their disrespect with calm authority, not aggression. You might say, *I don't allow myself to be spoken to that way. If you want to continue this conversation, it needs to be respectful.* Then, you pause. You don't argue, you don't plead, you simply stand in your truth. In that moment, you model strength. You show them that love and respect are inseparable, and that your worth is not up for negotiation.

The Sister Who Always Has a Crisis When You Level Up

The timing is uncanny. Just as you're on the edge of expansion, she unravels, pulling the spotlight back to her. Sometimes those closest to us seem to create "emergencies" right as we rise. Our compassionate side says, *be there for her,* while our power protector rises to stand guard.

The key is presence without collapse. Love doesn't always mean stepping off your path; it often means staying on it so others can see what's possible.

A boundary here might sound like: *I care deeply about what you're going through, and I also need to honor what needs to be done in my own life. Let's connect when I can be fully present."* This acknowledges the struggle while keeping your trajectory intact and gives you time to regroup, plan, and think about the best outcome.

One woman I coached had a sister who would call at all hours of the night, every conversation a swirl of chaos and crisis. Eventually, my client set a boundary: "I love you, but I need to sleep at night. Please call me during the day instead."

The next week, the phone rang at midnight. Her sister hadn't changed. And this is where most women stumble; they assume the boundary failed because the other person didn't honor it. **But here's the truth: The boundary isn't proven in their response; it's proven in *yours*.**

Instead of answering, my client let the call go to voicemail. The next morning, she sent a loving text: "I saw you called late last night. I need my rest, so I didn't pick up. I'm available to talk today after 2 p.m."

In that moment, she wasn't punishing her sister; she was training herself to honor her own schedule. Over time, the late-night calls stopped, not because her sister suddenly transformed, but because my client stopped collapsing her own boundary with false guilt. Remember, guilt is an indicator that you did something wrong. Many times, we confuse guilt with feeling bad about a situation.

This is the heart of boundary work: The power doesn't lie in their compliance; it lies in your consistency.

The Loved One Who Withholds Praise or Masks Digs as Jokes

"Not every boundary needs words. Sometimes the most powerful 'no' is the energy that refuses to shrink, explain, or over give."
~ Theresa Ream

Few things sting more than having your glow ignored or mocked. Their silence or sarcasm cuts deeper than open criticism. The unspoken message is clear: *don't shine too brightly.*

I have a client who recently lost a significant amount of weight. She's glowing, radiant, healthy, confident in ways she hasn't felt in years. And yet, her husband never acknowledges how incredible she looks. No compliments, no recognition, not even a casual, "You look great." His silence is deafening. It's as if by withholding praise, he's trying to keep her anchored in the old version of herself. This is what withholding does; it erodes joy by making you question whether your victories are visible and or viable.

Some loved ones withhold praise as a subtle form of control, training you to perform harder for crumbs of validation. Others mask their discomfort with digs disguised as humor: "Don't get too full of yourself," or "Well, you finally did something right." These comments sting because they are meant to shrink you while pretending to be "just a joke." Naming them breaks the spell. You can calmly say, "That doesn't land as funny for me," or "I don't find jokes at my expense amusing." Bringing the behavior into the light dismantles its power.

But your response is never to dim; it is to stay radiant. Celebrate yourself openly. Dress up, beam in the mirror, post the picture, toast yourself. A response might be, "That doesn't feel respectful or loving. Can we start over?" This is both boundary and invitation. You're not shaming them; you're showing them how you expect to be treated while modeling your feminine power.

The best advice I can give you around nurturing your power is to surround yourself with women who will celebrate you without hesitation. Their reflection reminds you of the truth: Your shine is not negotiable.

Each of these boundaries is not about punishing others; they are about **protecting your energy, your joy, and your power that controls your destiny.**

They are rivers that guide love to flow in ways that sustain rather than drain you.

Alignment Tools

1. Anchor in Who You Are Now

Before responding to anyone who knows your past, quietly remind yourself who you are today. Your growth does not require validation. When you are anchored in your present identity, their comments lose their ability to pull you backward. This inner grounding prevents old dynamics from reactivating and keeps you standing in adult sovereignty rather than slipping into a child role.

2. Respond Without Defending

Defensiveness drains power. You do not need to explain, justify, or prove yourself to be valid. Simple, neutral responses like "I hear you" or "I'll think about that" keep the interaction calm while protecting your energy. Feminine power is composed, not reactive. When you stop arguing for your worth, you quietly reinforce it.

3. Create Emotional Space Without Cutting Love

Distance does not have to mean disconnection. Sometimes protecting your power means limiting how much access someone has to your inner world. You may choose not to share certain goals, dreams, or decisions with those who consistently question or minimize them. This is not punishment; it is discernment. Love can remain while access is adjusted.

4. Reclaim Authority Internally

The deepest boundary happens inside you. When someone's words sting, pause and ask yourself, *What authority am I giving them right now?* Then consciously take it back. Affirm your truth internally, even if you say nothing externally. Each time you choose self-trust over old approval patterns, you strengthen your feminine leadership and weaken the sniper's influence.

Boundaries Are Your Feminine Fortress

Boundaries are not walls that block intimacy; they are invitations into a higher frequency of love. They are how you train the world to treat you. They say: *This is the sacredness of my life. Meet me here, or not at all.*

Every time you say yes to something that dims you, you say no to your destiny.

Every time you collapse to keep the peace, you abandon yourself.

Boundaries reclaim the balance. They are not about others; they are about you.

And here's the mistake so many women make: They believe that once a boundary is spoken, the other person will automatically honor it. But that is not how it works, especially with those who have a history of stomping boundaries. When you place your sacred life in their hands, you are giving away the very power you are trying to protect.

Boundaries are not contracts for other people to keep; they are commitments you make to yourself. **It is not *their* job to enforce them; it is *yours*.**

Subtle boundary stompers, silent sniper, emotional sniper, boundary stomper, the silent withdrawer, the perpetual victim, the withholder, the hurtful "joker" and the crisis king or queen will always test your lines. But your boundaries are the walls of your temple. They do not keep love out; they protect the sacredness within.

When you draw them, you're not pushing people away; you're inviting them into the truest, most luminous version of you.

Subtle boundary stompers don't always announce themselves with disrespect or demands. They often arrive wrapped in concern, charm, or humor. They might say, "I know you're busy, but you're so good at this ..." or "Don't take this the wrong way, but ..." They test the edges of your space with small requests, emotional weight, or assumed access to your time. You'll notice them not by what they say, but by how you feel after the interaction: slightly drained, defensive, or unsure of whether you're allowed to say no. When your body tightens, your chest sinks, or your mind starts rehearsing excuses, it's not overreaction; it's your intuition alerting you that a line has been crossed.

Subtle boundary stompers rely on your politeness, empathy, or desire to keep the peace. They know you value harmony, so they push just enough to make you question yourself. The giveaway is the energetic imbalance that follows—you leave the conversation over-explaining, apologizing, or carrying emotional labor that isn't yours. Feminine power calls you to notice this early, not with anger, but with awareness. The moment you feel yourself shrinking, pausing your truth, or softening your "no," pause and reclaim your center. Boundaries don't need to be shouted; they can be silently embodied, a calm knowing that says, *I see what's happening, and I choose not to participate.*

Here's the sacred truth: Your job is not to fix them. Your job is to stop abandoning what's right for you.

Boundaries are the most radical form of self-love. They're not about changing others; they're about declaring who you are and what you will no longer tolerate.

Your power does not need to roar; it only needs to stand. You were born powerful, and your boundaries prove you finally believe it.

"Feminine power doesn't shout its boundaries; it embodies them. The moment you stand in self-trust, the world quietly rearranges around your energy."
~ Theresa Ream

Action Plan: Protecting Your Power

1. Diagnose the Leaks

Goal: Notice where energy is draining before it becomes a pattern.

Do: After any unsettling interaction, jot quick notes:

- What was said/not said?
- Where did it land in my body (tight chest, jaw, stomach)?
- What is the *simplest* boundary that would have protected my power?

Power Reframe: "My body's signal is wisdom, not overreaction."

2. Name the Sniper, Not the Person

Goal: Separate behavior from identity so you can respond cleanly.

Do: Identify the *behavioral archetype* you're facing:
- **The Withholder** (praise/affection withheld)
- **The Silent Withdrawer** (distance used as control)
- **The Historian** (anchors you to an old version of you)
- **The Crisis King/Queen** (creates emergencies when you rise)
- **The Guilt-Trip Artist** (equates your boundary with a lack of love)
- **The Subtle Boundary Stomper** ("You're so good at this ... could you just take care of it for me?)

Power Reframe: "This is a pattern, and patterns can be retrained. It is not my fault."

3. Choose Your Boundary Type before the Next Interaction

Goal: Match the boundary to the leak.

Do: Time Boundary

"I'm available between 2–4 p.m."

A time boundary protects your calendar and your capacity. It communicates that your time is intentional, not endlessly flexible. Feminine leadership honors rhythm and focus. When you define when you are available, you prevent resentment, burnout, and last-minute urgency from dictating your life. Time boundaries are not rigid. They are respectful agreements with yourself first, and with others second.

Do: Access Boundary

"No business calls after 7 p.m."

An access boundary defines when and how people can reach you. It protects your personal space, family life, and nervous system. Without access boundaries, others assume constant availability. With them, you train people to respect your presence and your priorities. Access boundaries are not about shutting people out. They are about ensuring you show up rested, clear, and fully available when it truly matters.

Do: Topic Boundary

"I don't discuss religion, finances, or politics."

A topic boundary protects your mental and emotional energy. Not every conversation deserves your engagement. When certain subjects consistently create tension, drama, or unnecessary conflict, you are allowed to decline participation. This is not avoidance. It is discernment. Choosing which conversations you enter keeps your leadership focused on what aligns with your values and purpose.

Do: Tone Boundary

"I speak and receive with respect."

A tone boundary sets the emotional standard of your interactions. It communicates that disagreement is acceptable, but disrespect is not. You do not need to match aggression with aggression. Calmly stating your expectation for respectful communication reinforces your self-worth without escalating conflict. Tone boundaries elevate conversations rather than suppressing them.

Do: Energy Boundary

Silent non-participation; you don't explain, you redirect.

An energy boundary is often invisible but powerful. It is the decision not to engage in gossip, chaos, manipulation, or emotional dumping. Instead of arguing or over-explaining, you simply decline to participate. You change the subject, shorten the interaction, or remove yourself from the dynamic. Energy boundaries protect you and preserve your influence. Sometimes the strongest boundary is the one you do not announce.

Power Reframe: "Boundaries are rivers that guide love where it can flow."

4. Use Clear Scripts—Practice out Loud

To the Historian (parent/old friend):
"Thank you for caring. I've grown, and I trust my choices now. I'd love your support in celebrating this."

To the Silent Withdrawer (partner):
"I sense distance. I value our intimacy. I'm here for an honest conversation when you're ready."

To the Guilt-Trip Artist (adult child):
"I love you. My choice doesn't reduce my love, and I believe in your ability to handle this."

To the Withholder/Joker:
"That doesn't land as loving for me. If we continue, it needs to be respectful."

To the Crisis King/Queen (sister/friend):
"I care deeply, and I'm also honoring my moments. I can be fully present tomorrow at 3 p.m."

Power Reframe: "I'm not controlling *them*; I'm protecting what's important to *me*."

5. Enforce With Consistency, Not Drama

Goal: Remember that the boundary is proven by your follow-through.
Some examples are:

- If they call after hours, don't pick up. Text the next day with your window.
- If the joke lands as a dig, name it once; if repeated, end the conversation.

- If silence is used as control, hold your center. No chasing, no collapsing.

Power Reframe: "I train others by how I consistently respond."

6. Create a Home Energy Protocol

Goal: Make your space a sanctuary.
Some examples are:

- **Doorway ritual:** Hand on heart at the door, and repeat, "My home is a temple. My peace is non-negotiable."
- **Tech edges:** No conflict by text. No heavy talks after 9 p.m.
- **Visibility altar:** A small space with a photo, quote, or token of your becoming, reminding you who you are when someone speaks to your past.

Power Reframe: "My environment reflects the strength of my boundaries."

7. Build Your Circle of Celebration

Goal: Replace covert drains with overt amplifiers.
Some examples are:

- Choose three women who celebrate you without hesitation.
- Create a *Celebration Thread* (text/WhatsApp). Weekly share: one win, one boundary honored, one ask.
- Hold a quarterly brunch or Zoom, and ask: "What are you rising into next, and how can we support it?"

Power Reframe: "I am safest with women who don't require me to shrink."

8. Pre-Plan Your "No"

Goal: Remove on-the-spot guilt by pre-writing your declines.
Some examples are:

- "That won't work for me."
- "I can't, and I wish you the best in finding support."
- "I'm not available for that, but here's what I *am* available for ..."
-

Pair each "no" with a *self-yes*: a walk, bath, journal, text a friend, or nap to anchor the boundary somatically.

Power Reframe: "Every no to dimming is a yes to my powerful presence."

9. Repair Without Surrender When You Wobble

Goal: Give yourself grace while adjusting your response.
Some examples are:
You'll occasionally cave, over-explain, or answer the midnight call. Clean it up quickly:

1. **Acknowledge:** "I crossed my boundary."
2. **Reset:** "Going forward, I'll only discuss this during the day."
3. **Resume:** Act in alignment immediately.

Power Reframe: "Power is consistency, not perfection."

10. Track Your Power

To better track your power ledger, following are some brief explanations of the tracking terms.

What is a "leaky moment"?

A *leaky moment* is any moment where your personal power, energy, or authority quietly drains because a boundary wasn't fully honored. It's rarely loud or dramatic. Most leaks are subtle, habitual, and often well-intentioned.

A leaky moment might look like:

- Saying yes when your body clearly wanted to say no
- Over-explaining or justifying a decision you already knew was right
- Taking responsibility for someone else's emotions or outcomes
- Responding immediately when you needed more time
- Allowing guilt, urgency, or fear of disappointing someone to override your inner knowing

Leaky moments are not failures. They are *data*.

Body signals I honored

Your body is constantly communicating truth before your mind catches up. Body signals may show up as tension in your chest, a tight jaw, shallow breathing, fatigue, or a sudden sense of unease. They can also appear as calm, openness, relief, or a grounded yes. Honoring body signals means pausing when your body contracts, giving yourself space when you feel overwhelmed, and trusting the sensations that guide you toward safety, clarity, and alignment rather than pushing past them out of habit or obligation.

Consider an upgrade to expand your power
An upgrade is a small, intentional adjustment that strengthens your power. It might be a clearer boundary, a more honest response, better rest, asking for support, or choosing not to engage where your energy is drained. Upgrades are not about doing more. They are about doing one thing differently on purpose, based on what your body and awareness have already shown you. Each upgrade compounds over time, creating sustainable growth without force.

The Power Ledger
- **Kept boundaries:**

  ____

  ____

- **Leaky moment** (and what triggered it):

  ____

-
  ____

- **Body signals I honored:**

  ____

  ____

- **One upgrade for next week:**

  ____

  ____

What triggered it?
This part matters. Triggers often include:

- Feeling rushed or pressured
- Wanting to be liked or perceived as "easy" or "helpful"
- Old identity patterns such as caretaker, fixer, or peacemaker
- Fear of conflict, loss, or missed opportunity

Why we track leaky moments

Tracking leaky moments builds self-trust instead of self-criticism. When you can see *where* your power leaks, you can strengthen that place gently, without force.

Celebrate one *kept* boundary with something tangible (flowers, a drive by the beach, a latte date with yourself, a sunset drive). Embodiment cements the identity shift.

Mantras ~

- "My peace is not up for negotiation."
- "I won't abandon my truth to keep the peace."
- "Not every boundary needs words; my energy holds the line."

Remember: Boundaries are not punishments. They are love that's directed. And the moment you hold them with calm consistency; the world quietly rearranges around your energy.

Chapter Six: The Law of Feminine Flow— Dancing with Life's Rhythm

There is a river within you. It is not a river you must build, control, or dam. It is the river of your feminine essence, the flow that carries you toward the life you are meant to live. This flow comes from your higher power and flows from the unseen, through you, and out to the world.

When you are in flow, you are not straining against the current or scrambling to swim faster than everyone else. Instead, you are moving with the rhythm of your intuition, surrendering to the turns of the water, and trusting that the river already knows its way to the sea.

This is not about doing less or drifting passively; it is about aligning your energy so that life feels like a dance, not a battle. Flow is where feminine power shines: It is magnetic, easeful, and creative. And while it may look effortless, it requires trust, practice, and the courage to let go of control.

We have all had days when we were in flow, days when everything seemed to move with ease. Conversations landed effortlessly. Decisions felt clear. Time unfolded without resistance, and even challenges felt manageable. Then there are the other days. The days when nothing works, when every task feels heavy, and it's as if you are pushing life uphill inch by inch. It reminds me of the man condemned to roll a massive rock up a hill every day, only to watch it tumble back down again. On those days, effort multiplies but progress disappears, and so does our peace. The difference between these two experiences is not talent, intelligence, or discipline; it is alignment. Flow turns effort into ease. Resistance turns effort into burnout. And once you recognize that contrast, you begin to understand why honoring flow is not a luxury; it is essential to a life well lived.

Most women have lived for years, even decades, in the opposite state of flow: pushing, striving, forcing, hustling, and suppressing their natural rhythms. We've been taught that only through control, sacrifice, and sheer willpower do we deserve success. But feminine flow whispers another truth: when you release resistance and follow intuition, you not only reach your destination, but you also enjoy the journey along the way.

Flow Alignment: Releasing Resistance

"Flow turns effort into momentum. Resistance turns momentum into exhaustion."
~ Theresa Ream

Flow alignment begins with awareness. Before we can release resistance, we must first recognize it. Resistance rarely announces itself loudly. More often, it shows up quietly in the body and subtly in the mind. It feels like tight shoulders that never fully relax. A shallow breath you do not notice until it deepens. A constant sense of urgency or pressure to fix, prove, or push something forward. Resistance lives in the space where trust has been replaced by control.

Take a moment now to pause and turn your attention inward. Notice where your body feels tense or braced. Notice where you may be clenching emotionally or mentally. Resistance often reveals itself through effort that feels heavy rather than purposeful. It shows up when you are trying to make something happen before it is ready, or when you are judging yourself for not being further along. It can sound like self-criticism, comparison, or impatience with your own timing. You will also notice that you are sighing a lot. This is the body's natural response to release tension.

Resistance disconnects you from flow because it disconnects you from trust. When you are resisting, you are subtly telling yourself that this moment should be different, that you should be different, or that life has somehow gotten it wrong. Flow, on the other hand, begins with acceptance. Not passive acceptance, but grounded acknowledgment of what is here and now.

Now gently ask yourself what you may be resisting right now. Is it a situation that feels uncertain? A conversation you are avoiding? A season of rest you believe you have not earned? A transition you did not plan for? Simply naming it without judgment begins to loosen its grip. Resistance thrives on unconsciousness. Awareness alone starts to soften it.

Imagine what might happen if you released the need to fight *what is*. Not forever. Not completely. Just for this moment. What if instead of asking why something is not working, you asked what it is teaching you? What if instead of forcing clarity, you allowed it to emerge in its own time? Flow often returns not through action, but through permission.

Letting go is not the same as giving up. Letting go is a conscious choice to stop wasting energy on what you cannot control. It is choosing alignment over exhaustion. When you let go, you create space. Space for insight. Space for creativity. Space for life to meet you halfway. The river does not respond to force, but it responds beautifully to movement that works with its current.

As you release resistance, you may notice a shift. Your breath deepens. Your thoughts slow. The urgency softens into curiosity. This is flow returning. Flow does not demand that everything be easy or predictable. It simply asks that you be present and willing to listen. When you are aligned, even challenges feel more navigable because you are not fighting yourself along the way.

When you find yourself slipping back into resistance, begin with compassion. This is a lifelong practice, not a single decision. Each time you notice tension, see it as an invitation rather than a failure. An invitation to pause. To breathe. To realign. To remember that you do not have to push the river forward. You only must step into it.

Flow alignment is ultimately about relationship. Your relationship with time. With effort. With trust. With yourself. When you release resistance, you return to a state of partnership with life instead of opposition. You move from striving to allowing, from force to alignment, from depletion to renewal.

Let this reflection be a reminder that flow is always available to you. Not when everything is perfect, but when you are willing to soften. When you choose presence over pressure. When you remember that your power does not come from pushing harder, but from trusting deeper.

Intuition and Feeling as Your Guide

"Intuition is not a modern luxury; it is an ancient inheritance. God wired women with discernment long before strength was ever enough."
~ Theresa Ream

The masculine world teaches us to lead with logic. Strategy, planning, and execution are rewarded, while intuition and feelings are often dismissed as "irrational" or "emotional." But intuition is not a hindrance; it is one of the greatest expressions of feminine power.

Think about the last time you felt something in your body before your mind caught up. Maybe it was a hunch not to sign that contract, a gut feeling to call a friend, or the quiet inner nudge to rest when your calendar was full. That was your intuition speaking.

Feelings are not obstacles to overcome; they are signposts pointing the way. Your joy shows you what lights you up. Your frustration reveals where you are out of alignment. Your fear often signals the exact place you are being called to grow.

When you begin to treat your emotions as allies instead of enemies, you start to live in flow. Rather than ignoring your body's signals in favor of a to-do list, you tune in and ask: *What feels right in this moment? Where is my energy asking to go?*

A woman in flow is a woman who trusts her inner compass more than the noise around her.

From the very beginning, women were endowed with a highly tuned intuition for a reason. Long before modern life, long before systems and structures, survival depended on discernment. In early human history, women often did not have the physical strength of men, but they possessed something equally powerful: perception. The ability to sense danger before it appeared. To read subtle shifts in behavior. To feel when something or someone was not safe. This wasn't accidental; it was essential. God granted women intuition as a form of protection, a divine intelligence woven into the nervous system and the heart. While men often met the world through force, women learned to navigate it through awareness. That ancient knowing still lives in us today. When we ignore our intuition, we disconnect from a wisdom that has kept women alive, resilient, and perceptive for generations. When we honor it, we return to a sacred inheritance that was never meant to be silenced.

Flow Alignment: Honoring Your Intuition

Pause for a moment and return to your body. Before you analyze or explain anything, simply notice what is present. Your body holds information long before your mind organizes it into meaning. Take a slow breath and allow yourself to arrive fully in this moment.

Recall a time when you felt something was right or wrong before you had proof. Perhaps it was a quiet knowing, a subtle hesitation, or a calm certainty that did not need justification. As you remember that moment, notice what your body felt like. Was there tightness in your chest or shoulders, or a sense of ease and expansion? Did the feeling come with calm, urgency, warmth, or clarity? These sensations are not random. They are part of the language of intuition.

Now gently reflect on how you responded. Did you listen to that inner signal, or did you override it with logic, explanation, or fear? Many of us were taught to doubt what we feel and trust only what can be proven. Over time, this conditioning can quiet the very wisdom that was designed to guide us.

Bring your attention back to the present and ask yourself softly, without pressure or judgment, *Where in my life am I being invited to trust my intuition more fully?*

Allow one situation to come to mind, personal or professional, where your inner knowing is already speaking. You may feel it as a pull, a pause, or a persistent inner nudge. You do not need to solve it or act on it right now. Simply acknowledge that it is there.

Consider what might shift if you honored that guidance instead of questioning it. How would your body feel if you chose trust over doubt? How might your energy change if you allowed intuition to lead rather than asking it to prove itself?

Close this reflection by placing a hand on your heart and affirming: *I trust the wisdom God placed within me. I allow my intuition to guide me back into flow.*

Let this awareness move with you today, not as something to figure out, but as something to feel. Your intuition does not require explanation. It only asks for your attention and your trust.

Surrendering to the Process

Flow cannot be forced. The very act of trying to control it breaks the current.

Most of us were taught that surrender means failure. But in feminine power, surrender is the ultimate act of trust. It says, *I don't have to control every detail for things to unfold perfectly. I can allow life to work with me instead of against me.*

Imagine a dancer locked in rigid choreography. She hits every mark, but there is no life in her movement. Now imagine a dancer who lets the music move through her, improvising with trust and freedom. That is surrender.

When you surrender to the process, you stop fighting reality. You stop resisting the unexpected twist in your business plan or the detour on your personal path. You allow what is unfolding, trusting that every bend in the river is carrying you to where you are meant to be.

This does not mean you abandon goals or stop caring about outcomes. It means you soften your grip and release the illusion that you must make everything happen on your own. In surrender, you create space for miracles.

A Client Story: When She Stopped Forcing, Everything Moved

When Elena first came to me, she wasn't tired from lack of effort. She was exhausted from too much of it. Every decision felt heavy. Every outcome depended on her pushing, managing, or holding things together.

She believed that if she stopped forcing, everything would fall apart. The opposite was true.

For Elena, forcing meant over-explaining, over-planning, and constantly adjusting herself to keep momentum going. What she didn't see was that her effort was blocking movement. By gripping so tightly, she left no room for life to respond.

From the outside, she looked composed and capable. On the inside, she felt tight, anxious, and disconnected from the joy that once fueled her work. She was beginning to lose clients, not because she lacked skill, but because she wasn't connecting.

"I feel like I'm pushing a boulder uphill every day," she told me. "Even when I do well, it feels heavy."

In our work together, we introduced space. She learned to pause before defaulting to control, to trust what she already knew, and to stop rehearsing everything to perfection.

Conversations became easier. Opportunities arrived without chasing. Clarity replaced urgency. The same energy she had been using to push forward became available for listening, choosing, and responding.

The first time she let flow lead in a client meeting, she set aside her script and spoke from presence. She told a story instead of delivering bullet points.

During our next call, she said, "They listened more. And I didn't even try."

That was the turning point.

We then layered structure *around* her flow, not on top of it. Clear goals, healthy boundaries, and simple preparation rituals became a container for her intuition, not a constraint.

Within months, her work changed. Conversations became a two-way street of communication. Clients responded more quickly. Opportunities arrived without chasing. Most importantly, the exhaustion lifted.

"I didn't lose control," she reflected. "I gained trust in myself."

This is the paradox of feminine power. Force creates resistance. Presence creates flow. When women stop forcing and start allowing, while honoring direction and boundaries, power no longer feels heavy. It feels alive.

Embracing Vulnerability

To live in flow is to live open. But openness requires vulnerability.

Vulnerability is often misunderstood. Many women associate it with weakness, exposure, or emotional risk. We are taught, subtly and overtly, that strength means composure, self-control, and the ability to keep going no matter what we feel. From an early age, women learn to armor themselves. We smile when we are tired or hurt. We suppress anger to keep the peace. We swallow tears to avoid making others uncomfortable. Over time, this armor can look like success, but it feels like disconnection.

When emotions are suppressed, they do not disappear. They settle into the body and the nervous system. They show up as chronic tension, irritability, exhaustion, or numbness. What many women describe as burnout is not always the result of doing too much. Often, it is the result of feeling too little for too long. Flow cannot exist where emotions are denied, because flow depends on movement. Feelings are meant to move through us, not be trapped inside us.

Vulnerability is not the opposite of power. It is power in its most authentic and grounded form. It is when you allow yourself to express joy, grief, fear, disappointment, desire, or uncertainty, and stand in your truth. And truth is where connection lives: connection to yourself, connection to others, and connection to life itself. Vulnerability brings you back into your body and into the present moment, where flow naturally lives.

I have witnessed this in masterminds, retreats, and one-on-one sessions. Women who arrive accomplished, capable, and outwardly confident often believe their strength lies in holding everything together. They have learned how to perform with competence and resilience. Then something shifts. A tear falls. A long-held truth is spoken. In that moment, the energy in the room changes. Their presence softens and deepens at the same time. Their real power emerges, not through polished words or perfect composure, but through honesty and humanity.

Vulnerability opens the door to flow because it removes the dam of resistance. The energy that was once used to hide, manage, or suppress emotion becomes available for creativity, clarity, and connection. When you no longer need to pretend, your system and body relax. You become more present. You stop leaking energy through emotional control and start accessing a deeper sense of ease.

Living in flow does not mean being emotionally uncontained or sharing everything with everyone. Discernment still matters. Vulnerability is not about oversharing. It is about being honest with yourself first. It is about allowing emotions to be acknowledged, felt, and released rather than judged or suppressed. When you embrace vulnerability, you give yourself permission to be fully human.

And in that permission, flow returns.

Trusting Instinct

One of the most beautiful aspects of flow is instinct, the quiet, embodied knowing that bypasses the endless chatter of the mind. Instinct does not argue, justify, or over-explain itself. It simply arrives as a sense of clarity, a pull toward something, or a subtle inner stop sign. It is calm, direct, and often unmistakable when we are willing to listen.

When you are in flow, decisions tend to feel effortless. You say yes or no without agonizing over every possible outcome. You speak the right words in a conversation without rehearsing them in your head. You leap without needing every detail mapped out, because something inside you already knows the next step. This does not mean the decision is always easy, but it feels truly aligned with who you are. There is less inner debate and more inner alignment.

Instinct is often misunderstood as impulsive or emotional. In truth, instinct is deeply intelligent. It is not random. It is the culmination of your intuition, your lived experience, and your feminine wisdom working together. Every moment you have lived, every lesson you have learned, and every emotional nuance you have felt is stored in your body. Instinct draws from this reservoir instantly, without needing conscious effort.

This is why instinct often feels faster than thought. The mind analyzes. The body knows.

Think of a mother who wakes up seconds before her baby cries. She did not reason her way there. Her body responded before her mind caught up. Or think of an artist who picks up a brush and paints exactly what is needed without planning each stroke. Or a leader who senses when a conversation needs honesty instead of strategy. That is instinct in action. It is ancient, relational, and deeply human.

Many women have been conditioned to doubt this form of knowing. We are taught to trust data over feeling, logic over sensation, and external validation over inner guidance. Over time, instinct can become quiet, not because it disappears, but because it is repeatedly ignored. Rebuilding trust with your instinct is less about learning something new and more about remembering what has always been there.

When you allow instinct to guide you, life begins to feel lighter. You are no longer carrying the weight of constant over-analysis or the pressure to make perfect choices. You stop outsourcing your authority and start listening inward. Decisions may still require action and responsibility, but they are no longer fueled by fear or self-doubt.

Trusting instinct does not mean abandoning reason. It means allowing reason to support intuition, not override it. Instinct tells you where to move. Structure helps you move well.

As you deepen your relationship with instinct, you will notice moments of quiet confidence emerging. You trust yourself more. You explain yourself less. You move through life with a sense of inner steadiness that does not require constant reassurance.

This is flow expressed through instinct. It is the wisdom of your body and spirit leading the way, reminding you that you already know far more than you think.

When Flow Finally Found My Voice

"Flow begins the moment you trust what you already know."
~ Theresa Ream

For a long time, I believed preparation was the same thing as confidence.

When I stood in front of a room to teach or speak, I came armed with pages of notes, carefully written, thoughtfully ordered, meticulously planned. On the surface, it looked like professionalism. Underneath, it was fear dressed up as structure.

The moment I felt my chest tighten or my voice waver, I would retreat into the safety of the page. I would read instead of speaking. Perform instead of connecting. I told myself I was being responsible, polished, prepared. But what I was really doing was keeping my power at arm's length.

Everything I needed was already inside me.

Years of lived experience.

Hard-earned wisdom.

Stories etched into my bones.

And yet, I didn't trust myself to let it flow.

When you read, you stay in your head. When you flow, you drop into your body. And being in my body, being seen, felt, and fully present, felt far more vulnerable than hiding behind perfect words.

That's when Caterina, my speaking coach, changed everything.

After teaching a workshop, she gave me some feedback; it was gentle and polite, but it was the kind of clarity that cuts through illusion.

"You need to stop reading when speaking," she said. "You know what you're speaking about."

There was no room to argue. No room to explain. Just an invitation, and a challenge to trust myself.

In that moment, I realized something profound: I wasn't lacking skill or knowledge; I was lacking trust in my own knowing. I had confused control with competence and structure with safety.

So, I put the paper down at my next speaker's training that I attended with her and six other women.

My hands trembled at first. My breath caught. And then something else happened. My voice dropped into its natural rhythm. Stories surfaced without effort. Words arrived exactly when they were needed. I wasn't performing anymore; I was conversing. I wasn't reciting, I was remembering. I was easily releasing my wisdom.

Flow had been waiting patiently all along.

I didn't abandon structure that day; I simply spoke what I knew. Structure became the container, not the cage. Flow became the voice, not the risk.

And when I let it speak, something remarkable occurred: the room leaned in.

That was the day I learned that feminine power doesn't come from having everything perfectly scripted. It comes from trusting what lives within you to rise when you are present enough to allow it.

Flow didn't make me less prepared. It made me more real.

And real, I discovered, is what truly resonates.

Letting Go of Resistance

Resistance is the opposite of flow. It feels like trudging through mud: exhausting, frustrating, and joyless.

You know you are in resistance when you are clenching, controlling, or trying to make something happen that clearly isn't ready. You know it when you are criticizing yourself, comparing your pace to others, or shaming yourself for not being "further along."

Resistance disconnects you from your power because it disconnects you from trust.

The moment you let go, even just a little, flow returns.

Letting go is not the same as giving up. It is the courageous choice to stop fighting what *is* and open yourself to what *could be.* It is shifting from *Why isn't this working?* to *What is life trying to show me here?*

When you release resistance, you regain your energy, creativity, and clarity. You remember that you don't have to push the river; you only need to swim with it.

How I Stayed in Flow

There was a season in my life when everything I had built seemed to need me at once. The companies. The team. My family. My coaching clients. Everyone needed something, and I, being the capable woman I am, wanted to give it all.

It started slowly, that feeling of tightening: meetings running long, creative ideas drying up, my laughter replaced with lists. I could feel the weight of my own striving pressing down on me. I was pushing ... and the harder I pushed, the more life seemed to push back. I felt like life was very hard, like I truly was pushing a boulder up a hill or running through deep mud. I would often cry with exhaustion. All I wanted was to sit and do nothing. I wanted it all to stop!

One morning, I woke before the sun. The house was quiet—no emails, no voices—just me and my coffee under the early sky. The moon was still visible, faint but present, and I remember thinking: The moon doesn't get bothered by the howling of the wolves. She just flows with the cycles, sometimes showing us her fullness, sometimes going totally dark. She just is, and simply by being, she controls the tides that keep the entire earth alive.

That image shifted everything.

I realized that I had fallen out of *flow*. I was gripping outcomes, over-strategizing, trying to control every variable. Being bothered by things that I had no control over. I was running my feminine power through a masculine filter, forcing what needed to unfold with little or no power to do so.

I decided that morning I would practice surrender, not as weakness, but as wisdom.

I turned off the noise. I stopped checking my phone before I checked in with my intuition. At times, I even turned it off or silenced it. I began moving slower, letting my instincts, not my fear, decide what came first.

And something magical happened. Within a week, I started to feel energy move again. Conversations that had felt heavy became effortless. Ideas returned with ease. Opportunities I had been chasing began finding *me*. There were even days when I cleared my calendar completely and just did what came naturally for the day.

Flow came back, not because I worked harder, but because I finally stopped resisting what life was trying to teach me.

Staying in flow, I learned, is not about everything being perfect or predictable. It's about trusting that when I'm aligned—body, mind, and spirit—the right things will always find their way to me.

Now, whenever I feel that old tightening in my shoulders, the urge to control, to perfect, to prove, I breathe and remind myself: *You don't have to swim against the river. You don't have to push the boulder up the hill. You need only let life unfold and do your best.*

Flow Alignment: Releasing Resistance

Take a quiet breath and notice where you may be holding tension right now. Resistance often lives in the body before it shows up in our thoughts. It can feel like tight shoulders, shallow breathing, or a constant urgency to fix, push, or prove. Let yourself acknowledge where you have been forcing outcomes, judging your pace, or fighting what is unfolding. Without criticism, simply notice. Now imagine loosening your grip, even slightly. Ask yourself what might happen if you stop pushing the river and allow yourself to move with it instead. What would change if trust replaced control? Flow begins the moment you soften, when effort gives way to alignment, and you allow life to meet you where you are. Let this be a reminder that surrender is not failure; it is wisdom. And when you release resistance, you make room for clarity, creativity, and ease to return.

Flow Alignment Questions

- Where in my life am I pushing instead of allowing?
- What am I trying to control that may not be ready to move yet?
- Where do I feel tension, tightness, or urgency in my body right now?
- If I softened my grip just a little, what might change?
- What feels heavy because I'm forcing it, not because it's wrong?
- Where am I comparing my pace to someone else's instead of honoring my own rhythm?
- What would trusting the timing of my life look like in this moment?
- If I believed life was working *with* me, not against me, what choice would I make next?
- What is my intuition quietly asking me to release?
- How can I move with the river today instead of swimming upstream?

Mantra ~
"I do not force the river. I move with it."

Cultivating Feminine Energy

Feminine flow is not simply a mood; it is a power source.

A woman in flow radiates a magnetic energy that others feel immediately. People are drawn to her presence, not because she forces herself into the spotlight, but because she glows with alignment and ease.

She does not chase opportunities; they come to her. She does not beg for support; people offer it willingly. She does not collapse when setbacks come; she bends, shifts, and rises again with grace.

You can cultivate this energy through daily practices.

- **Stillness**—quiet moments of meditation, journaling, or prayer
- **Movement**—dancing, walking in nature, or yoga to move energy through the body
- **Expression**—speaking your truth, creating art, or sharing your feelings without censoring them
- **Connection**—spending time with women who uplift you, building circles of support, and nurturing relationships that align with your values

Every time you choose alignment over force, authenticity over performance, and intuition over obligation, you feed your feminine flow.

The Power of Intention: Creating Flow One Segment at a Time

"I release what was and choose how I enter into what's next."
~ Theresa Ream

Flow doesn't require a perfect day. It requires conscious transitions.

Most of us don't lose flow because of what happens to us, we lose it because we carry one moment into the next without pause. A hard meeting bleeds into the drive home. The drive home bleeds into our relationships. Before we know it, a single difficult hour has hijacked an entire evening.

This is where intention becomes one of the most powerful tools for flow.

Segment intention is the practice of setting an energetic intention for the *next part* of your day, rather than letting the previous one dictate what follows. It is the feminine art of choosing how you enter a moment instead of reacting from the residue of the last one.

For example, imagine a long, frustrating day at work. Your shoulders are tight, your mind is spinning, and you can already feel irritation rising. Without intention, it's easy to walk into your home carrying that energy, snapping at your husband, shutting down emotionally, or staying stuck in frustration long after the workday has ended.

But with intention, you pause.

Before you turn the key or open the door, you choose differently.

You set the intention: *When I walk into my home, I will hug my husband. I will speak gently. I will let this space be a place of rest, not release.* That single choice shifts everything. Your body softens. Your breath slows. Your energy changes. The evening unfolds differently, not because the day was easy, but because you were intentional.

This is flow in action.

Intentions act like energetic boundaries. They create a clean break between moments so one experience doesn't contaminate the next. You stop dragging the past forward and start meeting the present with clarity and choice.

Segment intention can be used anywhere. Before a meeting, set the intention to listen instead of proving your point. Before a difficult conversation, set the intention to stay grounded and compassionate. Before rest, set the intention to receive without guilt.

Flow is not about avoiding difficult moments. It's about meeting each moment fresh, unattached to what came before.

When you set intentions, you become the conscious creator of your experience instead of the emotional byproduct of your circumstances. And over time, this simple practice restores flow, not because life becomes perfect, but because you stop letting one moment steal the next.

Mantras ~
"I leave the past moment behind and step into this one with intention."
"I choose the energy I bring into this space."

Flow and Structure: A Sacred Partnership

"You were never meant to force your way forward. You were meant to flow, guided by trust and held by structure."
~ Theresa Ream

It is important to remember flow without structure becomes chaos. Structure without flow becomes rigidity. True feminine power is found in the dance between the two.

Feminine flow allows creativity, relationships, and opportunities to move freely. Masculine structure gives that flow boundaries, direction, and purpose.

Think of a river. Without banks, water spills aimlessly and loses its path. With banks, it gains momentum, direction, and force. The same is true in your life and business.

Too much flow without structure, and you may drift without focus. Too much structure without flow, and you may suffocate under rigidity. But when you balance them, you create harmony, ease paired with direction, intuition paired with strategy, surrender paired with strength.

Feminine leaders know how to integrate both. They honor their flow while creating structures that allow it to thrive.

Living in Flow

Living in flow is not a one-time achievement; it is a daily practice.

Each day you are invited to soften into trust, listen to your intuition, and allow vulnerability to guide you instead of fear. Some days you will succeed beautifully. Other days you will slip back into resistance and control. That is human. The practice is to notice, pause, and return to the river.

Flow is not about life being perfect, it is about you being present, open, and fully alive to the rhythm of what is unfolding.

When you choose flow, you choose freedom. You choose creativity over rigidity, presence over performance, ease over exhaustion. You choose to dance with life instead of battle it.

And in that choice, you discover the secret that women of power have always known: You do not have to force your way to your destiny. You must simply flow toward it with your aligned actions.

Practices for Flow

Flow Finds You When You Stop Chasing It

When I look back on that morning—just me, the moon, the quiet, and the remembering—I see how simple the shift truly was. Flow doesn't return because you fix things. It returns when you soften. When you stop proving and start allowing.

Staying in flow means choosing trust over tension. It's where your feminine power lives, not in hustle, but in harmony.

Every time I release the need to control, I return home to myself. That's when life becomes art again. The right people appear. The right ideas land. And instead of managing outcomes, I start magnetizing them.

When I lead from that space, my influence expands effortlessly. I become more radiant, more intuitive, more attuned to the rhythm that was always guiding me.

Because flow isn't something you find; it's something you remember. The connection never left you, all you need to do is plug back into your power source.

To bring this law into your daily life, try these feminine practices:

1. **Morning Check-In**
Before diving into your day, pause and ask: *What do I feel today? What does my body need? What one thing feels most aligned right now?* Let this guide your priorities.

2. **The Art of Pause**
When you feel resistance or frustration, stop. Breathe. Ask yourself: *Am I forcing this? What would flow look like here?*

3. **Dance with Your Emotions**
When strong feelings arise, don't suppress them. Put on music and move your body until the energy shifts. Let the emotion flow *through* you.

4. **Trust the Nudge**
Each day, act on at least one small intuitive nudge. Call the person who comes to mind, take the walk you feel drawn to, or say yes to the opportunity that excites (and often scares) you.

5. **Balance with Structure**
Create gentle boundaries, such as designated work hours, financial goals, or routines that allow your flow to flourish without overwhelming you. I structure a workout daily to hold my fitness practice because when you are fit, a lot of life falls into place naturally. I structure my life around time for friends, travel, and learning. I structure time for caring for my family and animals. I structure time for taking care of my home and cooking healthy meals, and I structure time to strategize around my business and life. And most importantly, I structure time for self-care.

This is the law of flow: When you dance with life instead of battling it, you become magnetic, powerful, and free. Flow is the feminine rhythm of life, and when you live in harmony with it, you discover that power was never about force. Power is about aligning your life with the seen and unseen forces.

Chapter Seven: The Law of Feminine Leadership—Leading with Grace

"Leadership is not about knowing the way; it is about trusting yourself enough to move without one."
~ Theresa Ream

Expansion, Influence, and Leadership

Pioneering Your Own Path

True feminine leadership is not about following a roadmap. It is about becoming the map.

There comes a moment in a woman's life when the path in front of her can no longer be traced from someone else's footsteps. She has learned the rules. She has studied the systems. She has proven she is capable, intelligent, and responsible. Yet something within her begins to whisper that the way forward will not be found by repeating what has already been done. This moment is not confusion; it is initiation.

When you step into the archetype of the pioneer, you walk a path that has never been walked before. There is no manual to consult, no proven formula to rely on, and no guarantee that the outcome will match expectations. You are asked to create reality from imagination, to build bridges where none visibly exist, and to trust that the next stone will rise beneath your foot only after you choose to move. Feminine leadership begins in this place of uncertainty, not because it lacks intelligence, but because it honors a deeper form of knowing.

This is the essence of feminine power. It is the courage to follow intuition even when logic hesitates. It is the willingness to say, *I may not have all the answers, but I trust where I am being led.* This trust is not blind. It is cultivated through listening, embodiment, and lived experience. It is a relationship with your inner compass, one that strengthens every time you choose alignment over approval.

This path is not an easy one. Feminine leadership asks you to dismantle the inner people pleaser, the part of you that learned to stay safe by staying agreeable. It requires you to risk being misunderstood and to remain rooted when others project their discomfort onto your expansion. You may be labeled too much, too sensitive, or too unconventional. Yet history reminds us that those who change the world rarely blend in. They lead with grace, conviction, and clarity without apologizing, not because they seek attention, but because they refuse to abandon themselves.

A feminine pioneer does not ask permission to step into her destiny. She claims it. She does not wait for validation to move forward. She follows the pull of her soul even when the path feels lonely, undefined, or downright scary. Her leadership does not rely on force, dominance, or control. It is expressed through inner frequency, through presence, through the coherence between what she believes and how she lives.

Each time you honor your intuition, new levels of courage awaken within you. Courage does not come before the leap. It arrives midair, in the moment you choose yourself. Power does not wait for certainty. It reveals itself when you say yes to the unknown and trust yourself enough to stay present through the unfolding.

Feminine leadership requires an inner surrender that many women have never been taught to value. It is the release of the need to control outcomes, to impress others, or to conform to expectations that no longer fit. This surrender is not weakness; it's living your truth. It is the recognition that your worth is not earned through performance but expressed through authenticity.

To lead from feminine power is to allow your inner truth to guide your outer action. This means listening to your body, honoring your rhythms, and respecting the wisdom that arises from stillness as much as from movement. It means understanding that leadership is not always loud or visible. Often, it is subtle, energetic, and deeply influential.

As a feminine leader, you notice that people respond differently to you. Conversations shift. Spaces soften and trust deepens. You no longer need to convince others of your authority because it is felt. Your presence becomes stabilizing, and your clarity becomes reassuring. Your alignment becomes contagious.

This kind of leadership does not seek to dominate or outperform. It seeks to elevate. It creates environments where others feel safe to step into their own power. It invites collaboration instead of competition. It honors both vision and humanity, strength and sensitivity.

When you embody feminine leadership, it is no longer something you do when the moment requires it. It becomes something you are in every interaction, every decision, and every boundary you set. It shows up in how you speak, how you listen, how you choose rest, and how you respond under pressure. It becomes woven into your identity rather than added to your resume.

Pioneering your own path means accepting that you will not always be understood by those who have not yet walked beyond the familiar. It means trusting that your way of leading will make sense not through explanation, but through embodiment. Over time, others will recognize the integrity of your path because of how it feels to be around you.

Feminine leadership is not about arriving at a destination where everything is resolved; it is about committing to a way of being that remains responsive, intuitive, and alive. It is leadership that evolves as you evolve, that deepens as you deepen, and that expands as you continue to choose truth over comfort.

When you lead this way, you are no longer imitating power; you are expressing it. Leadership becomes not something you strive for, but something you inhabit. And from that place, your impact is not only visible; it is both enduring and endearing.

How Expansion Happens Naturally

Feminine expansion unfolds like a blooming flower. It does not push its petals open or compete with the garden around it. It responds to light, nourishment, timing, and trust. In the same way, feminine leadership expands not through striving or comparison, but through rhythm and grace.

In the old paradigm, expansion was defined by more, faster, louder. More effort. More visibility. More urgency. Growth was something to be chased, conquered, and proven. But true influence does not come from hustle. It comes from harmony. Feminine power understands that sustainable growth happens in seasons. There are times of initiation and creation, times of nourishment and rest, times of harvest and visibility, and times of stillness and integration. Each season is necessary. None are mistakes.

When a woman leads from feminine alignment, expansion stops feeling forced. It begins to feel inevitable. Opportunities arrive without pursuit. Relationships deepen without manipulation. Influence grows not because she is trying to be seen, but because she is fully present where she stands.

This is how expansion naturally unfolds.

Presence over Persona

In traditional leadership models, success is often tied to image. Leaders are encouraged to curate themselves, to polish away rough edges, and to present a version of success that is impressive, controlled, and marketable. This creates performance rather than presence. It rewards appearance over authenticity.

The feminine leader chooses a different path. You release the need to perform success and instead commit to embodying truth. You allow yourself to be real rather than perfect. You show up grounded in who you are, not who you think you should be.

Presence is felt immediately. It softens rooms. It puts others at ease. It creates trust without explanation. When a leader is present, people feel seen rather than managed. They feel invited rather than evaluated.

Your team, clients, and community trust you not because you have all the answers, but because you are honest. They see your brilliance and your humanity coexisting. They witness your clarity and your vulnerability held together with integrity. This kind of authenticity builds loyalty far deeper than any marketing strategy ever could.

Presence also allows for responsiveness. Instead of reacting from habit or fear, the feminine leader listens. You notice what is needed now, not what worked before. This attentiveness allows your leadership to remain alive, relevant, and attuned. Expansion flows naturally from this state because people want to follow someone who is fully present.

Purpose Anchoring

Purpose is the soil from which sustainable power grows. Without it, expansion becomes scattered and exhausting. With it, growth feels rooted and coherent.

A feminine leader filters every commitment through a simple but sacred question: Does this align with who I am and what I value? This question becomes your compass. It guides your yes and your no. It protects your energy. It clarifies your direction.

When purpose is clear, distractions lose their grip. Opportunities that are not aligned fall away without drama. The fear of missing out dissolves because you understand that not everything is meant for you. Growth becomes less about chasing every possibility and more about magnetizing what belongs.

Purpose anchoring also brings consistency. Even as projects evolve and roles shift, your core values remain steady. People trust you because you are predictable in the ways that matter. You do not betray your principles for short-term gain. You do not abandon yourself to keep momentum.

This creates a powerful form of expansion. One that is stable rather than erratic. One that builds over time rather than burning out. Purpose allows growth to feel spacious instead of frantic. It keeps leadership aligned with meaning rather than metrics alone.

Invitation, Not Imposition

Feminine leaders do not command. They invite.

In masculine systems, leadership often relies on authority, compliance, and control. Decisions are imposed. Direction is enforced. Participation is expected. While this can create short-term efficiency, it often erodes trust and creativity over time.

The feminine way leads differently. It creates spaces where people feel inspired to step in rather than obligated to comply. It values choice, collaboration, and shared ownership.

In business, this looks like inviting input instead of issuing directives. It looks like collaborative strategy sessions where voices are heard and ideas are shaped together. It looks like leadership that asks questions rather than delivering constant answers.

In relationships, invitation shows up as curiosity instead of control. The feminine leader does not manage others' emotions or outcomes. She remains open, present, and engaged without coercion. This allows connection to deepen organically.

Invitation expands influence because people participate more fully when they feel respected. They bring their creativity, their insight, and their commitment because they want to, not because they must. This creates cultures and communities that are resilient, adaptive, and alive.

The feminine way opens the circle wider rather than building higher walls. It understands that true power grows through inclusion, not exclusion.

Steady Courage

Expansion is rarely comfortable. Growth stretches identity. Visibility invites scrutiny. Leadership often brings resistance, both internal and external.

Feminine courage is not loud or aggressive. It does not need to prove itself. It is steady. It is rooted. It is the quiet strength that stands firm when challenged.

This kind of courage is embodied. It lives in posture, breath, and presence. When storms arrive, the feminine leader does not panic or harden. She grounds. She listens. She responds from truth rather than fear.

You may be doubted. You may be dismissed. You may be challenged by those who are uncomfortable with your expansion. Feminine leadership does not require you to fight these moments. It asks you to remain anchored in who you are.

Over time, this steadiness becomes evidence. People watch how you hold yourself under pressure. They feel the calm you carry. They sense the integrity of your leadership. Trust grows not because you defended yourself, but because you stayed true.

Steady courage allows expansion to unfold without collapse. It keeps the leader intact as growth accelerates. It ensures that influence is built on substance, not reaction.

Growth of Others as the Metric

The feminine measure of success is not how high did she climb; it is how many rose with her.

Traditional leadership often centers on individual achievement. Titles, recognition, and personal milestones become the primary markers of success. Feminine leadership widens the lens. It understands that power multiplies when shared.

A feminine leader measures expansion by the growth she cultivates in others. She notices who is stepping into confidence. Who is finding their voice. Who feels supported enough to take risks and grow.

She invests in her people. She mentors. She listens. She creates opportunities for others to shine. Not because it benefits her image, but because it aligns with her values.

This creates exponential expansion. When others grow, the whole system strengthens. Teams become more capable. Communities become more resilient. Leadership becomes distributed rather than centralized.

The true legacy of a feminine leader is not found in what she built alone, but in what continues to grow because of her influence. It lives in the women she empowered, the teams she strengthened, and the lives she touched along the way.

Feminine leaders understand this truth deeply. Power is not diminished when shared. It is amplified.

Expansion as a Living Process

Natural expansion is not linear. It does not move in straight lines or predictable timelines. It ebbs and flows. It asks for patience, trust, and attunement.

When you lead from feminine alignment, you stop forcing growth and start allowing it. You honor the seasons of your life and leadership. You rest without guilt. You act without urgency. You trust that what is meant for you will find you when you are ready to hold it.

This does not mean you become passive. It means your action is informed by wisdom rather than fear. You move when the moment is right. You pause when integration is needed, and you listen as much as you initiate.

Expansion becomes a living relationship rather than a fixed goal. It evolves as you evolve and deepens as you deepen. It reflects the truth that leadership is not about arrival, but about alliance.

When a woman leads this way, growth stops feeling like pressure and starts feeling like expression. Her influence spreads not because she is trying to expand, but because her presence invites others to rise.

This is how expansion happens naturally.

Leadership Practices to Cultivate Radiant Influence

"Your inner sage lives in the body's senses, not in the analytical mind."
~ Theresa Ream

Radiant influence begins as an inner state long before it becomes an external action. It cannot be manufactured through strategy alone, nor can it be sustained through force. It is cultivated through your connection with alignment. Feminine leaders understand this intuitively. They practice alignment with the same devotion that others practice productivity, knowing that how they feel shapes how they lead.

This type of influence is not about doing more. It is about being more open to what the truth is, not the story you make up in your head. When a woman leads from coherence within herself, her presence speaks before her words do. People feel it. They trust it. They respond to it.

These practices are not tasks to complete; they are ways of orienting yourself to leadership that allow influence to flow naturally.

Morning Reflection Ritual Begins with Alignment

The way you begin your day sets the frequency for everything that follows. Feminine leadership does not start with the inbox, the calendar, or the demands of others. It starts with the inner compass.

Rather than reaching for your phone or mentally rehearsing your responsibilities, begin by turning inward. Pause long enough to feel your body and your breath. Ask yourself what energy you want to carry into the day. Notice which value you are being called to lead from. Sense where presence is required instead of performance. Consider what can be released or simplified so your energy is used intentionally rather than scattered.

When you begin the day in alignment, everything you touch carries that frequency. Conversations will open, and decisions will become clearer. Your center remains steadier even when the day brings challenges.

Feminine leadership feels like a river of energy moving in you, a joy. That energetic river is not something you create; it is something you allow. Others sense it when you lead from feminine power. They feel calmer around you. More grounded. More open. This is radiant influence in motion.

When We Are Vulnerable, We Lead with Our Humanity

In many traditional systems, vulnerability has been treated as weakness. Leaders were expected to be composed, certain, and unshakeable. Feminine leadership reclaims vulnerability as a bridge rather than a liability.

To lead with vulnerably does not mean oversharing or seeking reassurance. It means telling the truth. It means sharing what you are learning, not just what you have mastered. It means admitting when you do not have all the answers and allowing curiosity to replace control.

This kind of honesty builds trust quickly. When leaders are human, others feel permission to be human too. Innovation flourishes because people are no longer afraid of making mistakes. Ideas flow more freely. Collaboration deepens. Loyalty strengthens.

Vulnerability does not diminish authority. It refines it. It replaces fear-based compliance with genuine connection. When a leader models authenticity, people follow not because they must, but because they want to.

Affirmation of Others Shares the Spotlight

Radiant leaders go out of their way to lift others up. In a world that often pits women against one another, the feminine leader becomes a mirror of empowerment.

She notices the quiet contributions. She names effort as well as outcomes. She celebrates success openly and generously. She reminds others of their brilliance, especially when they forget it themselves.

Affirmation is not flattery. It is recognition rooted in truth. It tells people they are seen. It acknowledges their value without comparison or competition.

This practice dismantles scarcity at its core. When you understand that another woman's light amplifies your own, rivalry loses its grip. Leadership becomes open rather than defensive.

When people feel affirmed, they show up more fully. They take ownership. They invest emotionally as well as professionally. A culture of affirmation creates environments where people grow, stay, and contribute with pride. You create buy-in from the teams and organization.

Structure with Purpose Protects the Sacred

Feminine leadership is not boundaryless compassion. It is love with structure.

Every powerful woman eventually learns that without boundaries, energy leaks. Without clarity, influence dissipates. Saying yes to everything may look generous on the surface, but it often leads to resentment, exhaustion, and diminished impact.

Purposeful boundaries protect what is sacred. They preserve your energy so it can be directed where it matters most. They ensure that your leadership remains aligned rather than forced.

Ask yourself where you are saying yes from obligation rather than authenticity. Notice which commitments drain more than they give. Consider how one clear *no* could create space for your most meaningful *yes*.

Boundaries are not about pushing people away. They are about honoring your capacity. When you respect your limits, others learn how to respect you as well.

Consider this, when faced with the choice between disappointing someone else and disappointing yourself, your duty is to disappoint someone else. This is not selfishness. It is self-respect. It is about honoring your truth. Most people who feel disappointed will adjust far more quickly than we fear, especially when they see that your choices lead to growth and stability.

When boundaries are clear, influence flows like a focused river rather than a scattered flood. Your leadership becomes more potent because it is intentional.

Feedback Loops Refine Without Shrinking

Feminine leaders invite feedback not to seek validation, but to strengthen connection and clarity. They understand that growth requires reflection, and reflection is enriched through relationship.

Asking for feedback from your team, peers, or clients opens dialogue. It signals humility and confidence at the same time. It says you are invested in your evolution without being dependent on approval.

Receiving feedback requires patience. It asks you to listen without defensiveness and to discern without collapsing. Feedback is not failure. It is calibration. It helps refine your signal, so your message and mission remain clear.

One of the most powerful distinctions I learned from my mentor, Caterina, is that not all feedback is created equal. Wise leaders do not open themselves to commentary from just anyone. Feedback is sacred information. It should come from trusted allies who understand your vision, respect your evolution, and are invested in your expansion rather than your diminishment.

This discernment is feminine wisdom in action. You refine without shrinking. You remain open without becoming porous. You listen deeply while staying rooted in your truth.

True feedback strengthens your leadership. It never asks you to abandon yourself. Instead, it helps you lead with greater coherence, clarity, and confidence.

Radiant Influence as a Way of Being

These practices are not separate from one another. Together, they create a way of being that makes leadership feel grounded rather than performative.

When you begin in alignment, lead with humanity, affirm others, protect your energy, and invite wise feedback, your influence becomes radiant. People feel safe in your presence. They trust your leadership. They rise alongside you.

Radiant influence does not require constant effort. It is the natural result of coherence between who you are and how you lead. When leadership is rooted in alignment rather than force, it becomes sustainable, magnetic, and deeply impactful.

This is embodied feminine leadership.

Integrating Feminine Leadership into Your World

Wisdom only becomes power when it's lived. Integration is the bridge between knowing and embodying.

Here's how to weave feminine leadership into the key realms of your life, including business, personal, community, and self.

In Business: Elevation over Domination

"When leaders rise by lifting others, businesses grow in both profit and purpose."
~ Theresa Ream

Feminine leadership in business transforms "command and control" into "collaborate and cocreate."

You elevate others by giving them ownership, voice, and vision.

You run meetings that begin with gratitude or presence, not panic.

You build businesses that are both profitable and purposeful.

People do their best work when they feel seen, trusted, and invited into ownership rather than managed through fear or urgency. Instead of tightening your grip, you widen the circle. You lead by elevating others into their strengths, giving them a voice in decisions, and allowing vision to be shared rather than hoarded. Power is no longer something you wield over others, but something you cultivate within the culture itself.

This kind of leadership shows up in the way you run your company day to day. Meetings begin with presence or gratitude, not panic or pressure. Conversations are grounded, direct, and human. You listen as much as you speak. You ask better questions instead of delivering constant directives. Accountability still exists, but it is paired with trust. Standards are high, yet people are supported rather than shamed. When challenges arise, you address them without domination, knowing that clarity and respect are far more effective than force.

Businesses led this way do more than perform; they endure, prosper, and serve. They become environments where people grow, stay, and contribute with pride. Profitability and purpose are no longer competing values; they reinforce one another. When people feel elevated rather than controlled, creativity expands, loyalty deepens, and results follow. Feminine leadership in business proves that the most powerful organizations are not built on fear or hierarchy, but on alignment, respect, and shared passion.

In Personal Life: Authenticity Over Obligation

"When a woman honors her truth, her relationships find their natural balance."
~ Theresa Ream

The feminine leader knows that leadership does not end when she closes her laptop. At home, she leads through authenticity by honoring her own needs, setting healthy boundaries, and creating a rhythm that sustains her. She no longer confuses love with self-abandonment or responsibility with resentment. Living from authenticity means giving from overflow, not depletion. When you model this, your relationships evolve from performance to presence.

This kind of leadership invites honesty instead of obligation. You speak what is true rather than what keeps the peace at your expense. You allow others to take responsibility for their emotions instead of managing them for comfort or approval. Over time, this creates relationships that are cleaner, calmer, and more respectful. By choosing authenticity in your personal life, you teach those around you how to meet you as an equal, not a role you are expected to play. The best part of this is the love and connectiveness that will permeate your life.

In Community: Service over Spotlight

Feminine leadership in community is not about being the star; it's about being the spark.

In community, feminine leadership shows up as steady presence rather than loud visibility. You contribute because it matters, not because it is noticed. You build bridges between people, ideas, and generations, often working quietly behind the scenes to ensure others feel included and supported. Recognition becomes secondary to impact. What guides you is not applause, but alignment with your values and a sincere desire to strengthen the whole.

This form of leadership creates communities that feel safe, resilient, and alive. When service replaces the need for spotlight, trust grows, and hesitant voices begin to contribute their special talent. Women feel empowered to lead in their own way, knowing they are supported rather than compared. Over time, the collective becomes stronger because leadership is shared, and the community evolves through cooperation, care, and shared purpose rather than ego and pride.

True service is when you lend your influence by uplifting others and not making it about yourself. Wisdom is shared and there is no need for competing. You speak up for what matters, even when it's inconvenient. And it's all about service.

In Self-Leadership: Sacredness over Self-Sacrifice

Perhaps the greatest form of leadership is the way you lead yourself.

A feminine leader honors her own sacredness, her intuition, her rest, her cyclical nature. She knows that the way she treats herself sets the tone for how the world treats her.

Power Reflection: Claiming the Path That Is Yours Alone

The most powerful leadership begins with how a woman leads herself: her boundaries, her rest, and her reverence for her own energy."
~ Theresa Ream

Every woman comes to a moment when she realizes her life is not a rehearsal of someone else's dream; it is her own masterpiece in progress.

This is the moment of reclamation. The moment you stop performing and start creating.

Ask yourself:

- Where am I still waiting for permission to live the life I already know is mine?
- If I trusted my inner compass, what would my next bold step be?
- What would I release if I chose courage over conformity?

Each time you act from intuition and experience rather than approval, your destiny expands. Each time you choose authenticity over acceptance, your leadership deepens.

Leading with feminine power is not the absence of fear; it is the insistence that your destiny matters more. It is feeling the fear and doing it anyway. This is what builds confidence. When those who follow you see you face fear, they gain confidence to do the same. Because the real reason we lead is to build other leaders.

Learning to Lead from a Place of Ease

There was a time early in my leadership journey when I believed power meant holding everything together through control. I co-owned multiple companies, managed teams, juggled family, and carried the unspoken belief that if I slowed down, everything would collapse. I thought leadership meant never showing weakness, always knowing the next move, always being the steady rock for everyone else.

But behind that mask of composure, I was exhausted. My neck had anxiety knots that made me miserable. My body was whispering what my mind refused to hear: *This isn't sustainable.* I was leading with force instead of flow. I was trying to prove my worth through effort rather than presence. Not only that, but I was neglecting my self-care to the point that I was making myself sick.

It all came to a head during a season when everything demanded more of me: business growth, team expansion, and personal commitments all colliding at once. I remember sitting in my car after a long day of meetings, staring at the steering wheel, realizing I had no energy left to give.

For the first time, instead of tightening my grip, I had to let go; it was too painful to hold on.

Letting go didn't look dramatic. It looked deceptively small. After never setting foot in a gym, at age fifty-seven, feeling out of shape and looking super frumpy, I signed up to for my first bootcamp-style workout, not to chase youth or prove anything, but because my body was asking to be honored. After a few weeks of being so sore and stiff that I could barely walk, I released the old story that self-care was indulgent or optional and something to earn after everything else was done.

That someday became now by pure necessity. That single decision became a turning point. Moving my body loosened more than tight muscles; it quieted my anxiety and reminded me that leadership lives in the body, not just the mind. As strength returned, so did clarity. I slept better. I reacted less. I began leading from steadiness instead of strain. And thirteen years later, I still honor that commitment, showing up consistently for boot camp on a regular basis, not as punishment or pressure, but as devotion to my body and confidence. That practice became a nonnegotiable rhythm of self-leadership. The more I cared for myself, the more powerful and present I became. That one act of self-honoring changed my entire life. I not only gained muscle but also the self-confidence to move toward the life I desired and the things that I thought were impossible for me to do.

Showing Your Humanity: Modeling Feminine Leadership in Real Time

Several years after learning to lead from alignment rather than force, I attended a women's speakers' retreat in Napa Valley, Calif. It was my first time traveling alone: no husband, no safety net, and unfamiliar faces. Just me, a suitcase full of clothes I wasn't sure I'd wear, and a heart full of nerves.

I don't like public speaking, so much so that the choice between death and public speaking seems like a viable choice to me.

When my turn came to stand in front of the room, my throat tightened, and my hands trembled. I had led multimillion-dollar companies, managed complex operations, and faced down more than a few disasters, but looking into the faces of ten supportive women terrified me.

As soon as I began to speak, my voice cracked. I laughed nervously, then felt tears streaming down my face. I wanted to run to my car and never see these women again. But instead, something beautiful happened. These women, who I hardly knew, surrounded and supported me. Yes, I was embarrassed, but I was also loved and held up.

I took a breath, pressed my hand over my heart, and told the truth: "I'm nervous because I've always believed I had to perform to be seen by a brother and two sisters who were much older than me, and right now I am going through a huge personal crisis with a family member."

The entire room softened.

Women nodded. A few teared up.

And in that moment, something magical shifted: connection replaced performance.

That day, vulnerability became my most powerful leadership tool. I didn't have to "command the room"; I simply had to be *real*.

What I didn't know then was that this retreat would become the beginning of lifelong friendships and collaborations. The women who saw me that day became my allies. They invited me to speak at other events, to join them on women's cruises, to cocreate new projects. Each opportunity came not because I performed flawlessly, but because I showed up authentically. Years later, the women in that room are still a big part of my support system.

Now, when I lead workshops or speak to rooms full of women, I often tell that story. I tell them that the woman who once shook behind the microphone now laughs, dances, and speaks with joy because she leads from her heart.

I learned that feminine leadership isn't about having the perfect plan; it's about having the courage to stand in your truth and invite others to do the same.

When a woman leads that way, she doesn't just inspire confidence; she gives others permission to come home to themselves.

It's not always grand or polished; sometimes it's messy, human, and beautifully real. But it's magnetic. It's alive. And it's contagious.

Closing Prayer

Breathe deeply. Feel the rhythm of your heart sync with the
pulse of the earth.
You were born for this, this moment, this calling, this leadership.
You are not here to blend in; you are here to stand out in service.
You are not here to follow; you are here to forge new paths.
You are not here to prove; you are here to *be*.
May you lead with grace.
May your confidence become your compass.
May your presence be your power.
And may every woman who meets you rise a little higher,
because you dared to shine.
~ Theresa Ream

Acknowledgments

First and foremost, I thank my husband, Terry. Thank you for being my rock, my mentor, and my steady presence through every season. You are my strong oak tree, offering shade, protection, and quiet strength when I need it most. Your belief in me has grounded me more than you will ever know.

To my children and grandchildren, you are my greatest teachers. Through you, I have learned patience, humility, joy, and the kind of love that continually stretches the heart. You remind me why growth matters and why becoming more is always worth the journey.

To my coaches who walked alongside me at pivotal moments, thank you for your guidance, your wisdom, and your willingness to see what I could not yet see in myself. Your support helped shape not only this work, but the woman behind it.

To my friends, my business girlfriends, and my travel buddies, what would I ever do without you? You have been my sounding boards, my laughter, my mirrors, and my companions in both adventure and truth. You remind me that power is sweeter when shared and life is richer when lived together.

This book carries pieces of all of you within its pages. Thank you for walking this path with me.

About the Author

Theresa Ream is a living embodiment of feminine power in action. Over the decades, she has built several multimillion-dollar enterprises under The Ream Companies banner, becoming the largest minority woman–owned restoration company on California's central coast and beyond. Her companies, Disaster Kleenup Specialists, FRSTeam Contents Restoration, Flooring America's Floor Store USA, Catt Leasing LLC, and Cypress Cabinets stand as testaments to her vision, discipline, and unshakable belief that women can lead industries without surrendering their truth.

As the founder of Feminine W.I.L.E.S., Lifestyle & Business Consulting and Feminine Power Guide, Theresa channels her gifts for organization, strategy, and nurturing leadership into guiding women entrepreneurs. She knows that systems and structures matter, but only when they serve the woman who leads them. Her guiding principle is simple and profound: You must build the woman to build the business. Theresa's wisdom extends to the delicate art of running multigenerational family-owned businesses, where legacy and leadership intersect. Recognized as Best Woman-Owned Business and Best Minority-Owned Business of Monterey by KSBW News and Union Bank and honored as Woman of the Year by the Professional Women's Network of Monterey, she has become a trusted leader, voice, and role model in both her community and her industry.

A speaker, three-time bestselling author, and podcast host of *Feminine Power Unleashed*, Theresa's work has been featured in *Marketing, Media & Money Magazine*, and her voice has become a favorite on stages and airwaves alike. Her calling is not just to help women scale businesses, but to help them reclaim their power, step into their presence, and lead with alignment. When she's not coaching or running her companies, Theresa is an avid reader, traveler, and lover of bootcamp-style workouts and long bike rides. She is also devoted to her family, raising her grandson, Cash, alongside her husband, business partner, and high school sweetheart, Terry.

www.femininewiles.net
https://www.facebook.com/theresa.ream.98
https://www.linkedin.com/in/theresaream

www.ingramcontent.com/pod-product-compliance
Lightning Source LLC
Chambersburg PA
CBHW051804050726
47598CB00006B/2417